This book belongs to:

. . . .

DK | Penguin Random House

THIS EDITION
Senior Editor Carrie Love **Project Editor** Kritika Gupta
US Senior Editor Shannon Beatty
Senior Art Editor Roohi Rais **Art Editors** Mohd Zishan, Eleanor Bates
Managing Editors Monica Saigal, Penny Smith **Managing Art Editor** Ivy Sengupta
Deputy Art Director Mabel Chan **Publishing Director** Sarah Larter

PREVIOUS EDITION
Project Editor James Mitchem **Senior Designer** Lisa Robb
US Editor Rebecca Warren
Edited by Sophia Danielsson-Waters, Hélène Hilton, Violet Peto
Designed by Charlotte Milner, Hannah Moore, Claire Patané,
Samantha Richiardi, Sadie Thomas
Design Assistance Eleanor Bates, Rachael Hare
Fact Checker Gill Pitts
Pre-Production Producer Dragana Puvacic
Senior Producer Isabell Schart
Jacket Designer Charlotte Milner **Jacket Coordinator** Francesca Young
Creative Technical Support Sonia Charbonnier
Managing Editor Penny Smith **Managing Art Editor** Gemma Glover
Publisher Mary Ling **Art Director** Jane Bull

This American Edition, 2023
First American Edition, 2016
Published in the United States by DK Publishing
a division of Penguin Random House LLC
1745 Broadway, 20th Floor, New York, NY 10019

Copyright © 2016, 2023 Dorling Kindersley Limited
24 25 26 27 28 10 9 8 7 6 5 4 3 2 1
003–333852–Aug/2023

New material only
PA Reg. No. 14954 (CN)
Content: Polyurethane Foam

A catalog record for this book
is available from the Library of Congress.
ISBN 978-0-7440-8050-6

DK books are available at special discounts when purchased in bulk
for sales promotions, premiums, fund-raising, or educational use.
For details, contact: DK Publishing Special Markets,
1745 Broadway, 20th Floor, New York, NY 10019
SpecialSales@dk.com
Printed in China

www.dk.com

MIX
Paper | Supporting
responsible forestry
FSC™ C018179
www.fsc.org

This book was made with Forest
Stewardship Council™ certified
paper – one small step in DK's
commitment to a sustainable future.
**Learn more at www.dk.com/uk/
information/sustainability**

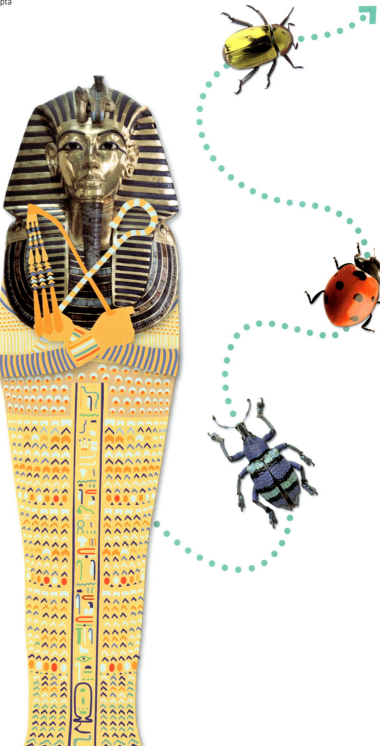

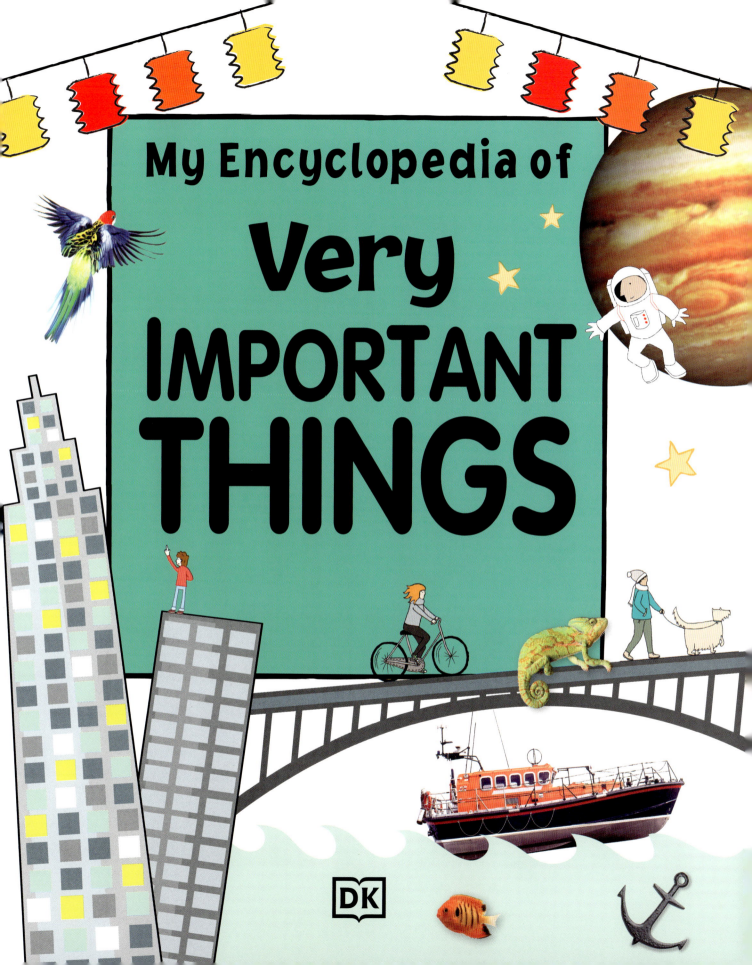

My Encyclopedia of
Very
IMPORTANT
THINGS

DK

Contents

Here are some **other** very important things

Very important things about

my planet

Earth is our amazing home. It's covered with lush forests, dry deserts, and big blue oceans (so big that Earth looks blue from space.) Earth is the only planet that we know of where things can live, so it's a **very special** place!

Our place in space

Our planet (Earth) is in a group with seven other planets. This group is called the **solar system.**

What are planets?

Planets are big round objects in space. Some are made of rock, and the others are big balls of gas. Most of them **orbit** (travel around) a star.

We live here

The sun

The sun is a star. Without its heat, no plants, animals, or people could survive on Earth. That includes you!

Huge rocks float between Mars and Jupiter in an area called the asteroid belt.

Earth

Mercury

Mars

Venus

The solar system is so big even the planets that seem close to each other are VERY far apart.

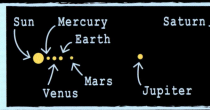

Sun   Mercury   Saturn
              Earth

Venus   Mars   Jupiter

The rings of Saturn are made of ICE and DUST.

Neptune

Uranus

Uranus is different to the other planets, because it spins on its side.

Saturn

It would take many, MANY years to reach the edge of the solar system.

All the planets SPIN as they move around the sun.

As far as we know, Earth is the only planet anywhere where things live.

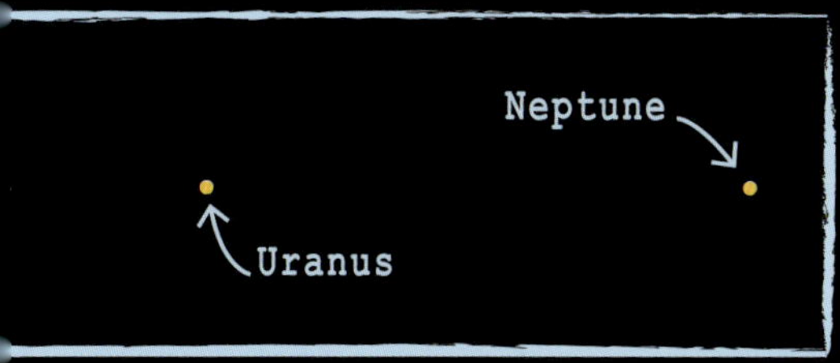

Jupiter

Neptune

Uranus

Our Earth

Earth is **our planet**. Most of it is covered by oceans. The rest of the planet's surface is land.

The Earth takes a whole year to orbit (move around) the sun once.

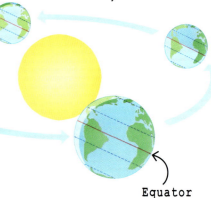

Equator

When the side of the Earth you live on faces the sun, it's daytime.

Where does the sun go at night?

The Earth is always spinning. As it does, the sun shines on different parts of the planet. This is why we have days and nights.

The Earth takes 24 hours to make one spin.

The equator is an imaginary line around the middle of the Earth. Think of it like the Earth is wearing an invisible belt!

When the side of the Earth you live on turns away from the sun, it's nighttime.

Inside the Earth

There are **three layers** under the Earth's outer layer (**crust**), but it's too hot for us to go there.

Mantle

Outer core

Inner core

The crust makes up all the land and the sea floor.

What's inside?

The **mantle** is almost solid rock, the **outer core** is liquid metals and minerals, and the **inner core** is solid metals and minerals.

If the Earth were an apple, the crust would only be as thick as the skin.

Which way is space?

If you could drive a car straight up, it would only take about an hour to reach space. On the way you'd pass through five layers of gases called the **atmosphere**.

Satellite

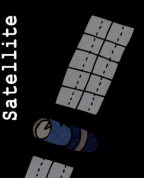

Satellites orbit the Earth all the way up here. They send signals to the world.

The top layer of the atmosphere doesn't end suddenly. It **fades** gradually farther into space.

Scientists say **space** starts here. This layer goes up really, REALLY high above the Earth.

Auroras

You can see the colorful aurora light show from places near the North or South Poles.

International Space Station

The Space Station is so big you can sometimes see it from the ground.

Exosphere

Thermosphere

Meteors

Brr! The air up here is **freezing** cold. The top of the mesosphere is the coldest place in the world.

Nacreous clouds
These beautiful clouds are very rare.

This area is home to the **ozone layer**, which helps protect us from the sun's rays.

Rüppell's vulture can fly higher than any other bird.

Jet planes fly above the clouds to avoid bumps caused by wind.

Airplane

Hot-air balloon

This is the lowest part of the atmosphere. All **weather** happens in this bottom layer.

Mesosphere   Stratosphere   Troposphere

The sky at night

Astronauts can stay at the International Space Station while they are in space.

If you look up on a clear evening, the sky can be full of twinkling lights. But not all of these are stars.

The moon is only visible because it reflects light from the sun.

The moon

The moon is an object that orbits planet Earth. There's nothing in the night sky that's easier to spot than the moon. Astronauts have walked on the moon. Their footprints will stay there for millions of years because there is no wind or weather there.

Phases of the moon

Have you ever wondered why the moon seems to change shape? It's because the sun's light hits the moon at **different angles** as it moves around Earth. There are 8 main phases.

New moon

Waxing crescent

First quarter

Waxing gibbous

Full moon

Waning gibbous

Last quarter

Waning crescent

Space station

Aircraft

Satellite

Meteor

Comet

Star

Planet

Moon

Here the moon is in
the *second phase*
(waxing crescent).

Eye to the sky
Telescopes help us to see
objects that are very far
away, such as planets.

Searchlights

Under the waves

From the surface to the sea floor, the oceans are packed with life. We can separate the ocean into four **zones**.

Let's go diving and learn about each one.

Lots of fish and other sea creatures are very colorful.

Look at the colors! Most sea creatures live near the surface because they need **light** and **warmth** from the sun.

Jellyfish

Sea horse

Sunlit zone

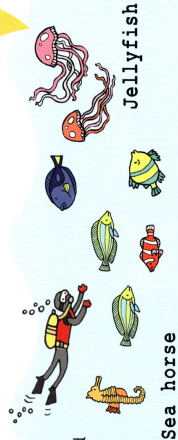

Whale

Giant sperm whales dive deep for food, then swim all the way up to the surface to breathe!

Brrr! Deeper down it gets **colder** and **darker**. Plants don't grow here because there isn't enough sunlight.

Twilight zone

Dumbo octopus

Angler fish

I have a spine on my head which I light up to lure prey. Then I suck them into my huge mouth and clamp my terrifying teeth shut!

Going deeper still, there are even fewer animals. Those that do live here are specially **adapted** for the cold and the dark.

The only way people can travel here is in special submarines.

NAUTILE

Gulper eel

The **deepest** parts of the ocean are so dark and hard to reach that even the smartest scientists don't know very much about them!

Midnight zone

Hadal zone

Mountains

Rising up from the ground, **MIGHTY** mountains rise into the sky. The peaks shown here are the **seven summits**, which are the highest peaks on each of the seven continents.

Mountain animals have adapted to life on steep and rocky slopes.

I'm off to the summit! That's what we call the top of a mountain.

3
Denali
(North America)

This giant mountain is the highest peak in North America.

6
Vinson Massif
(Antarctica)

There are huge mountains under the sea, too.

What makes mountains?

Over millions of years, the plates (sections) that make up the Earth's crust crash into each other, pushing the ground upwards. However, not all mountains get formed this way. Some can also be formed due to volcanic activity.

Plates start to push together.

Imagine the VIEW from up here!

1 Everest (Asia)

2 Aconcagua (South America)

4 Kilimanjaro (Africa)

This isn't just a mountain—it's a rift valley volcano too!

5 Elbrus (Europe)

This mountain is found in Russia.

7 Kosciuszko (Australia)

After a long, long time, mountains rise up!

The plates keep pushing, which make folds in the Earth.

21

Very fiery
volcanoes

Volcanoes are mountains with a fiery **surprise** inside. When it's eruption time, red hot **lava** bursts out, creating a breathtaking (but dangerous) sight.

Lava is very, VERY hot.

Eruptions throw ash and dust high into the air.

Eruptions

Volcanoes can go years and years without erupting. We call these volcanoes **dormant**. Others are erupting all the time!

What is lava?

Lava is fiery **melted rock** from deep within the Earth that has burst out from inside a volcano. It's so hot it destroys everything in its path.

Lava travels downhill for a long way before it hardens and cools.

Giant rock thrown from a volcano.

Most volcanoes are actually found under the **sea**. When they erupt, the lava can build up and form **islands**.

Shake and **quake**

Earthquakes are the **rumbling** and **shaking** of the Earth. Most of the time they are harmless, but sometimes they are very destructive and dangerous.

Puzzle planet

The Earth might seem like one huge rock, but it's actually made up of moving pieces called **plates** that connect together like a jigsaw puzzle.

Plate

Richter scale

Earthquakes are measured on something called the "Richter scale." The higher the number, the more powerful the earthquake is.

Low (1)

Weak earthquakes happen all the time, but most are too small for people to notice them.

What's the cause?

When Earth's plates rub together the pressure can cause an earthquake and shake the land above.

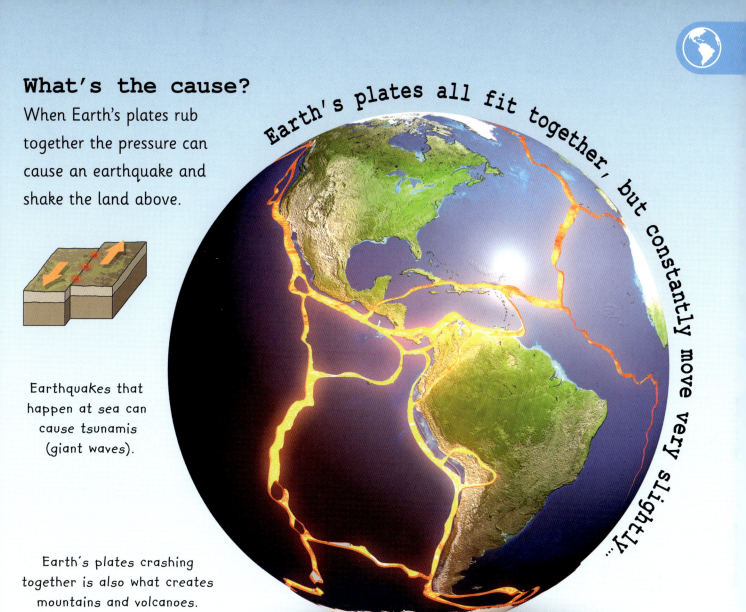

Earth's plates all fit together, but constantly move very slightly...

Earthquakes that happen at sea can cause tsunamis (giant waves).

Earth's plates crashing together is also what creates mountains and volcanoes.

Medium (4)   High (9)

Strong earthquakes can knock over trees and buildings, and can be very dangerous.

25

Dry as a **desert**

Deserts are very dry places that don't get much **rain**.
And without water, life can be very TOUGH.

Not much can grow in deserts because there's so little water, but cacti are plants that can store water in their trunks, which helps them survive there.

Hot deserts

Deserts aren't much fun for people. In places like the **Sahara** in Africa they have to put up with sandstorms, extreme heat, and a lack of food and water.

There are deserts all over the world,

The Atacama in South America is so **dry**, some parts haven't had rain in millions of years.

A lot of Australia is covered in a desert called the **Outback**.

Optical illusions

An **oasis** is a place in a desert where water is found. It is very rare and sometimes not even real! It can be an illusion created by the light called a **mirage**.

A penguin? Is that a mirage as well?

Brrr! Not all deserts are hot. Antarctica is a HUGE desert, and it's absolutely FREEZING.

and on every continent except EUROPE.

The Mojave in the USA is home to **Death Valley**. It doesn't have a nice name because it's not a nice place to be—it's really, REALLY hot.

Antarctica is the world's largest **cold desert**. There's lots of ice but very little rain or snow.

Rain forests

Also known as jungles, rain forests are thick, green forests full of **plants** and **animals**.

Those animals must not mind getting wet, because it **rains** a lot in these forests.

Rain forests can have lots of heavy thunderstorms.

The world's lungs

Rain forests are sometimes called the "lungs of the world." The trees help absorb carbon dioxide from the air and turn it into **oxygen**, which all living things need to breathe, including you!

It's the huge amounts of rain that makes rainforest trees grow so tall.

Rain forests are home to lots of plants and animals that don't live anywhere else.

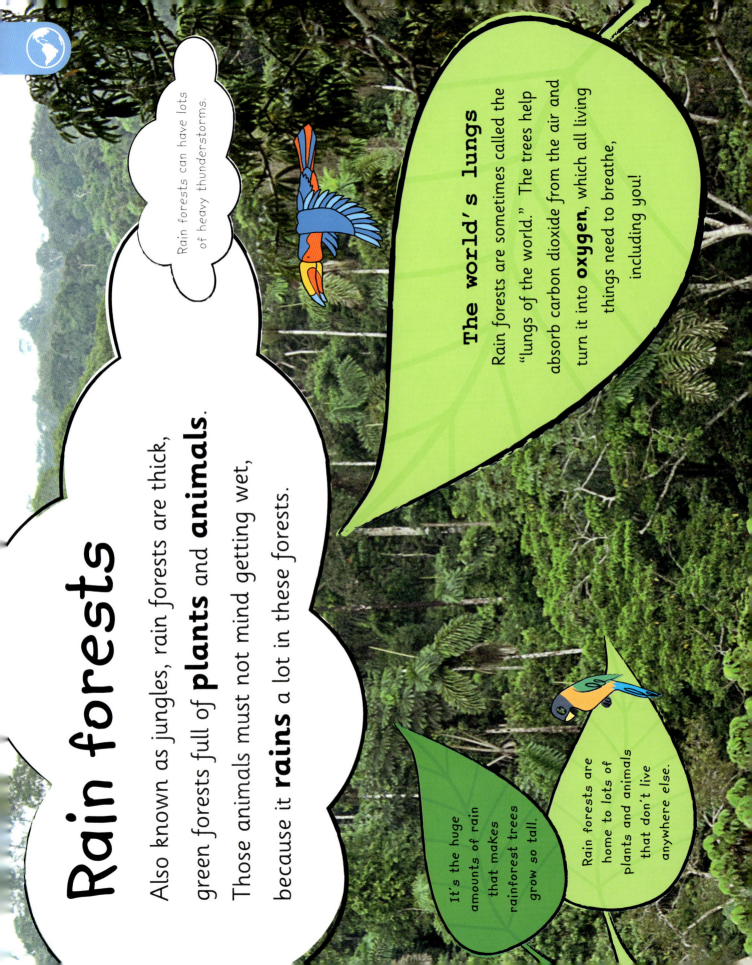

Rain forests are usually warm and very damp.

Tropical rain forests only grow near the Earth's equator.

The forest floor is so dark because the trees block out so much of the sunlight.

Almost half of all plant species on Earth live in rain forests.

Land of layers

Rain forests are made of separate layers. There's the **forest floor**, and **understorey**, which are full of small trees and animals. Above them are the **canopy**, tangled tops of trees, and the **emergent layer**—where the tallest trees stick out of the top.

Emergent layer

Forest floor

Wonderful water

Our planet is covered in water. It's in the sea, on the land, and in the air. The journey of water is called the water cycle.

2 The wind blows the vapor over land. When the vapor reaches cooler air, it turns into droplets of water. The droplets join together to make clouds.

1 The sun heats the sea and turns the water into **vapor**. The vapor rises into the air.

Most of the water on Earth is seawater, which is too salty to drink.

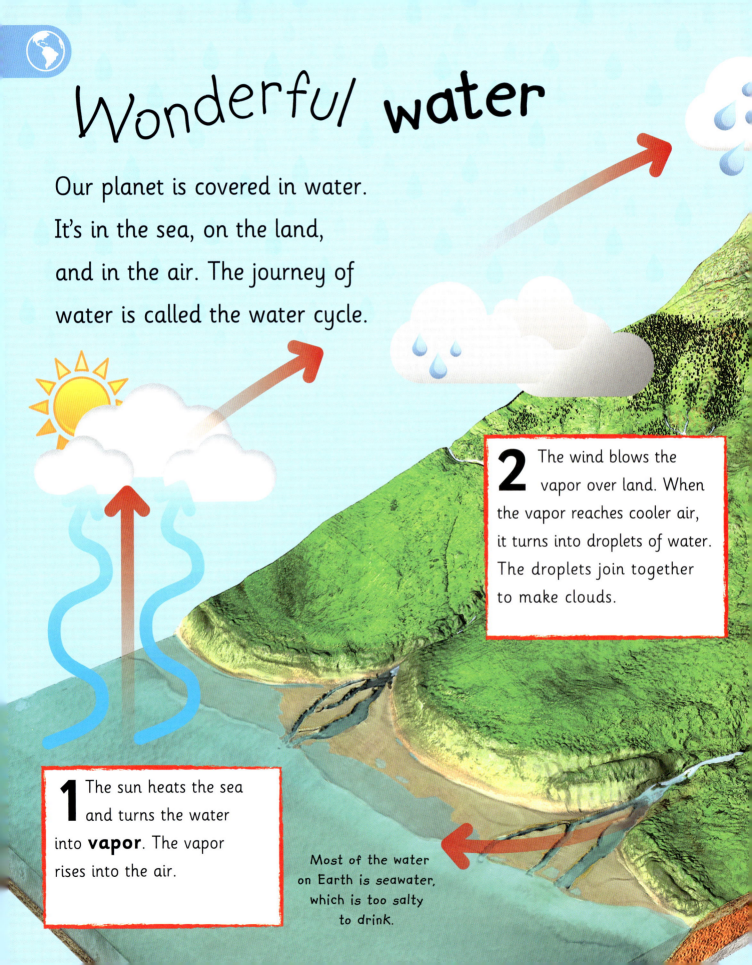

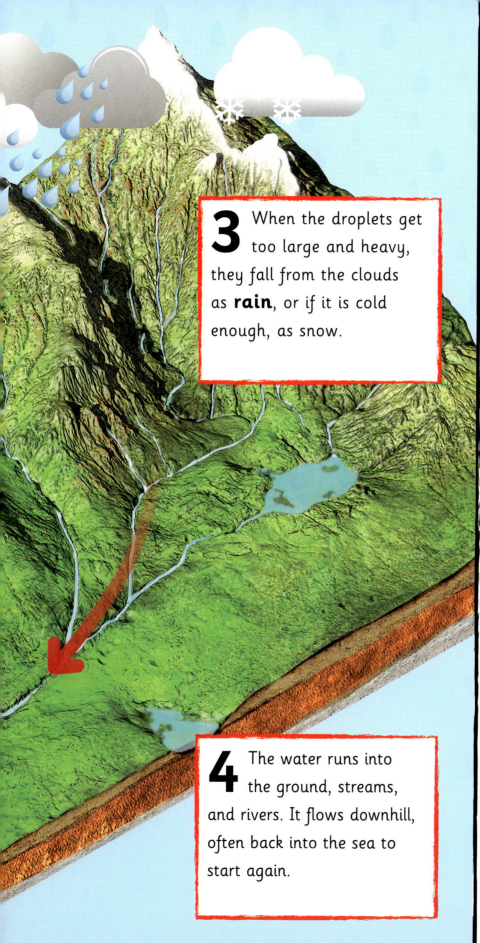

3 When the droplets get too large and heavy, they fall from the clouds as **rain**, or if it is cold enough, as snow.

4 The water runs into the ground, streams, and rivers. It flows downhill, often back into the sea to start again.

Water states

When water is heated up or cooled down, it can change from liquid into gas or solid ice. We call these different forms **states**.

When ice gets warm it melts and turns into water in its LIQUID form.

When water gets very cold it freezes into ice. This is water in its SOLID form.

When water gets hot it turns into steam (vapor). This is water in its GAS form.

How does it grow?

With enough time, teeny tiny **seeds** turn into giant plants. It's like **magic** in slow motion.

Sunflower seeds are here.

Roots

Seed

1
A sunflower head is full of **seeds**.

2
The seeds are **scattered** by birds who eat these and later drop them.

3
Rain and sunshine help the seed sprout and grow roots.

Big and small
Seeds come in lots of shapes and sizes. Some are bigger than your head, and others are almost too small to see!

The **coco de mer** tree has seeds that are as big as basketballs. "Coco de mer" means "sea coconut."

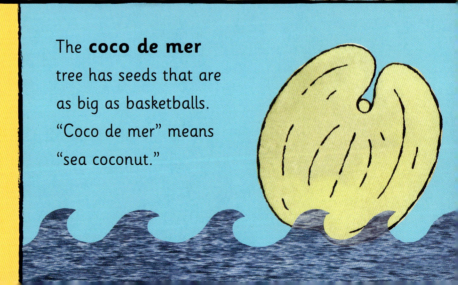

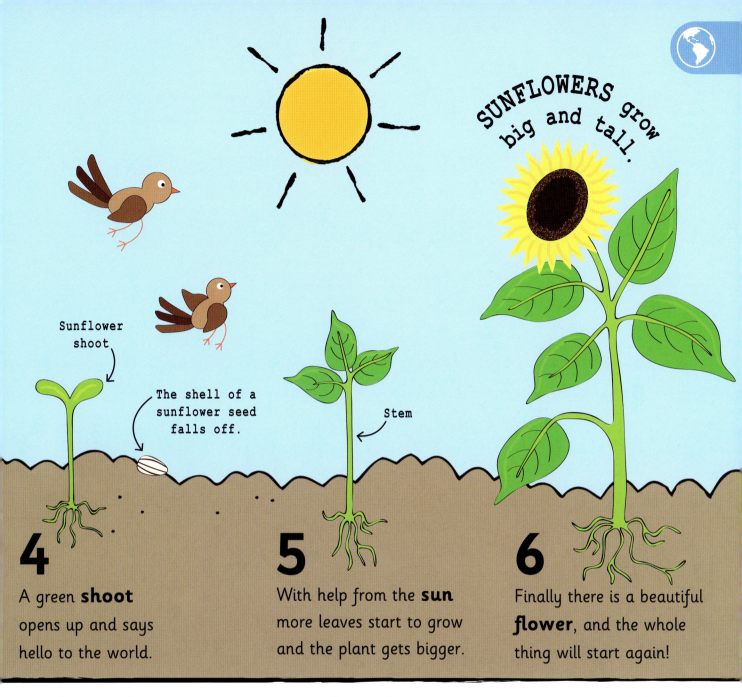

SUNFLOWERS grow big and tall.

Sunflower shoot

The shell of a sunflower seed falls off.

Stem

4 A green **shoot** opens up and says hello to the world.

5 With help from the **sun** more leaves start to grow and the plant gets bigger.

6 Finally there is a beautiful **flower**, and the whole thing will start again!

CAN YOU see where the SEEDS are in these FRUITS?

Tomato

Peach

Strawberry

Apple

The changing **seasons**

Each year, Earth goes through **times of change** that affect the weather, plants, and animals. These are known as seasons.

Spring

Spring can bring sunshine and rain, which helps plants and trees start to bloom.

Summer

Usually the warmest season, summer is the time crops and fruit grow the most.

Lots of animals have babies or lay eggs in spring.

Summer is a great time of year for animals and plants.

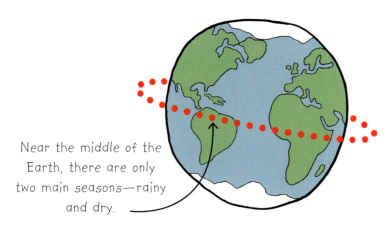

Near the middle of the Earth, there are only two main seasons—rainy and dry.

Why it happens

The seasons change as the Earth **moves around** the sun and tilts toward or away from it. So the season you are having depends on where you live on the planet.

Fall

In fall, the weather gets colder and some trees start to lose their leaves.

Winter

There is less sunshine in winter so it is much colder. Some animals sleep all winter long.

During fall leaves often change color.

During winter the days are darker and shorter.

Extreme weather

Crazy, weird, or **WILD**, sometimes it seems that weather has a mind of its own. When weather is extreme, that means it's different than normal weather.

Heat waves

This is what happens when it's **hotter** than usual. It makes the ground dry up and can cause fires.

Floods

When there's too much **water** and it has no place to go, you may get destructive floods.

Tornadoes

Super fast winds with a spinning center become twisty tornadoes that **swirl** and **WHIRL**.

What is climate change?

Climate change is the long-term shift in temperatures and weather. The way we live is changing the Earth's climate—it is becoming warmer. This change is leading to frequent extreme weather conditions.

Hurricanes

These heavy monster **storms** of wind and rain are also known as cyclones or typhoons.

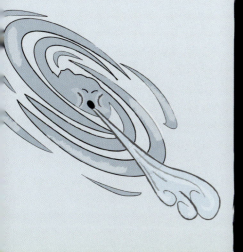

Lightning

Bolts of **electricity** are made inside clouds. They rush to Earth, striking tall buildings and trees.

Thunder

BOOM BOOM BOOM

This is the very loud **BOOMING** sound that lightning makes as it races through the air.

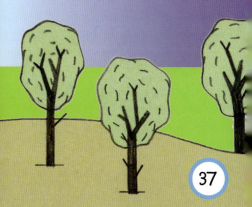

The Wind and the Sun

High up in the sky, the Wind was arguing with the Sun about which of them was **stronger**.

"I can make storms and hurricanes! You are quiet and weak," laughed the Wind.

"Being kind and calm is also a strength," replied the Sun.

So they decided to have a **contest** to see who could make a man take off his coat first. The Wind thought he'd win **easily**.

The Wind **huffed and puffed** with all his might. The man's coat flew open but did not blow off. The Wind blew harder but the coat stayed on.

When it was the Sun's turn, she **smiled** and began to **slowly warm** the Earth. The man smiled back and took off his coat to enjoy the weather.

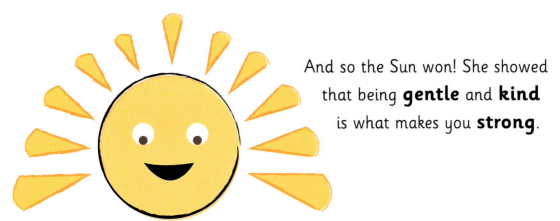

And so the Sun won! She showed that being **gentle** and **kind** is what makes you **strong**.

Very important things about

places

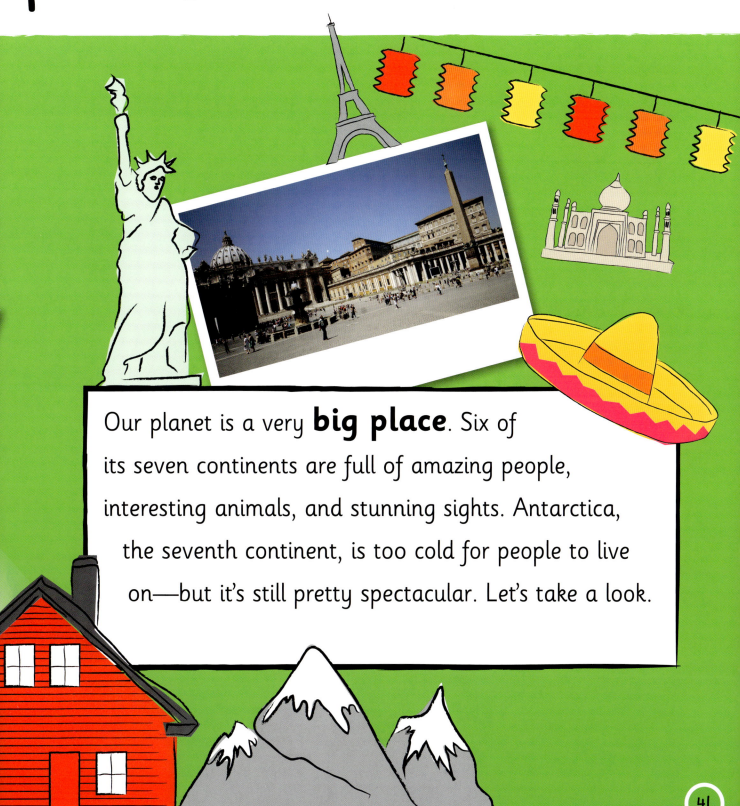

Our planet is a very **big place**. Six of its seven continents are full of amazing people, interesting animals, and stunning sights. Antarctica, the seventh continent, is too cold for people to live on—but it's still pretty spectacular. Let's take a look.

I can count **7** continents

Time to fly around the world and visit the continents. These are the world's **seven** big areas of land. Ready? **Let's go!**

There are more than 20 countries in North America.

1
North America

Bright lights at night

This is what the continents would look like from space if it were night everywhere. All those **lights** are busy cities!

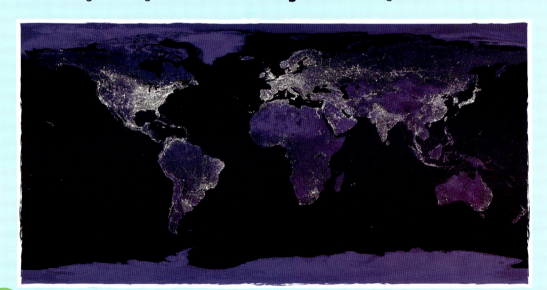

2
South America

Asia is the BIGGEST continent.

4
Europe

5
Asia

More than half of
the people in the
world live in Asia.

3
Africa

6
Australia

Brrr! Antarctica is
the driest, emptiest,
and coldest place
on Earth.

7
Antarctica

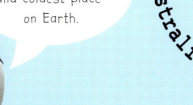

Australia is the SMALLEST continent.

Postcards from North America

There are 23 countries in North America. They can be hot, cold, small, or BIG, but they're all full of **interesting** people and places.

Pacific Ocean

Las Vegas, NV, has huge hotels and spectacular sights. It may be a big, bustling city, but it's also in the middle of a desert!

The "Day of the Dead" is an important event in Mexico. People wear colorful costumes.

Life on every Caribbean island is different, but there's always plenty of sun and lots of beautiful beaches.

This island is called Greenland. It's very cold!

Atlantic Ocean

Canada is the largest country in North America.

CANADA

Space Needle

Mount Rushmore

New York

UNITED STATES OF AMERICA

Las Vegas

MEXICO

The USA has the most people in North America.

El Castillo

Caribbean islands

People say New York City, NY, "never sleeps" because there's always so much going on.

Postcards from South America

The Amazon rain forest is full of animals. It's so big it covers parts of nine countries.

Rain forests, rivers, and mountains are just some of the things you'll see on this **amazing**, beautiful **continent**.

Amazon Theater

PERU

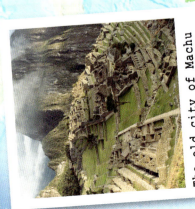

The old city of Machu Picchu, Peru, is a tourist attraction. People hike up the mountains to see it.

Christ the
Redeemer

Atlantic
Ocean

Cathedral of
Brasilia

Rio de
Janeiro

BRAZIL

Every year there is a lively
carnival in the Brazilian city
of Rio de Janeiro.

Although many languages, such as
Quechua and Italian, are spoken in
South America, Spanish is the
official language of many countries.
People in Brazil speak Portuguese.

BOLIVIA

Buenos
Aires

N   E
W   S

Pacific
Ocean

When it rains on the salt
flats of Bolivia, there
is an amazing mirror
effect on the ground.

Buenos Aires is the capital
of Argentina. It has many
colorful buildings.

Postcards from **Africa**

Africa is bursting with **life**.

It has rain forests and deserts, many countries, millions of people, thousands of languages, and astonishing animals.

MOROCCO

The Sahara Desert is huge, hot, and dry.

Sahar Deser

Atlantic Ocean

Marrakesh in Morocco is sometimes called the Red City because many of its buildings were built using red sandstone.

Chocolate is made from the cocoa beans inside cacao pods. They grow in West African forests.

N
W E
S

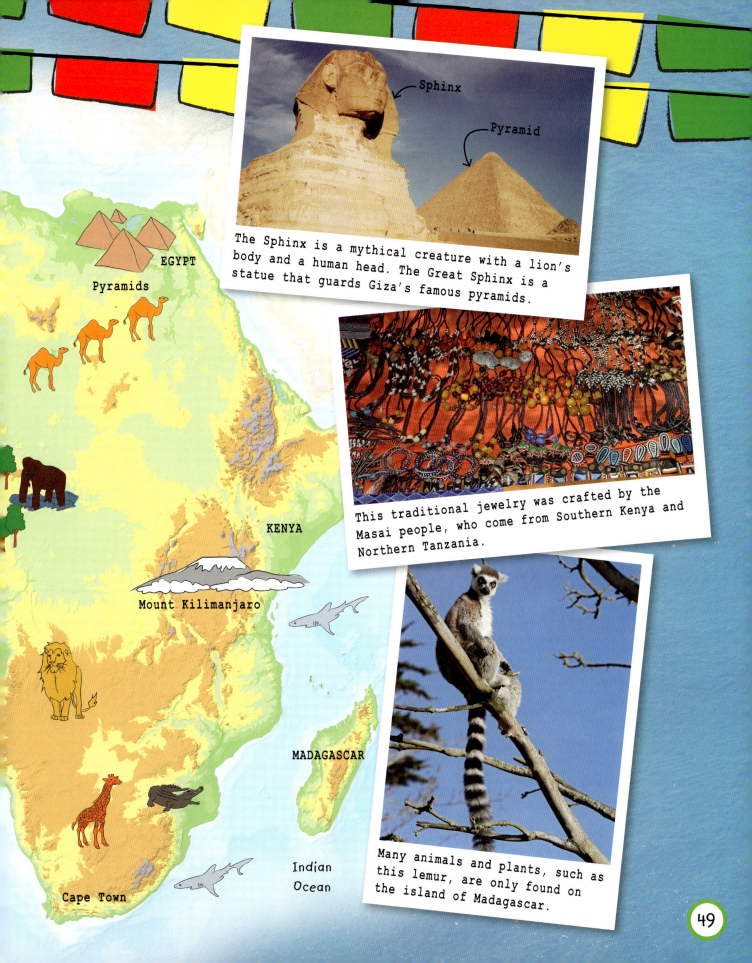

Sphinx

Pyramid

The Sphinx is a mythical creature with a lion's body and a human head. The Great Sphinx is a statue that guards Giza's famous pyramids.

This traditional jewelry was crafted by the Masai people, who come from Southern Kenya and Northern Tanzania.

Many animals and plants, such as this lemur, are only found on the island of Madagascar.

EGYPT

Pyramids

KENYA

Mount Kilimanjaro

MADAGASCAR

Cape Town

Indian Ocean

Postcards from **Europe**

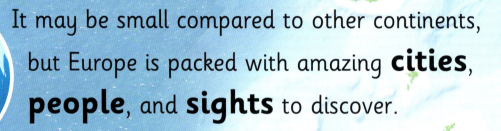

It may be small compared to other continents, but Europe is packed with amazing **cities**, **people**, and **sights** to discover.

Stonehenge in England is a huge mystery! It was built thousands of years ago from giant stones. Nobody knows for sure how or why it was made.

Based in the city of Rome in Italy, the Vatican is the world's smallest country. It's the home of the Pope, the leader of the Catholic Church.

Atlantic Ocean

Big Ben

Eiffel Tower

The Alps

Rome

N

W E

S

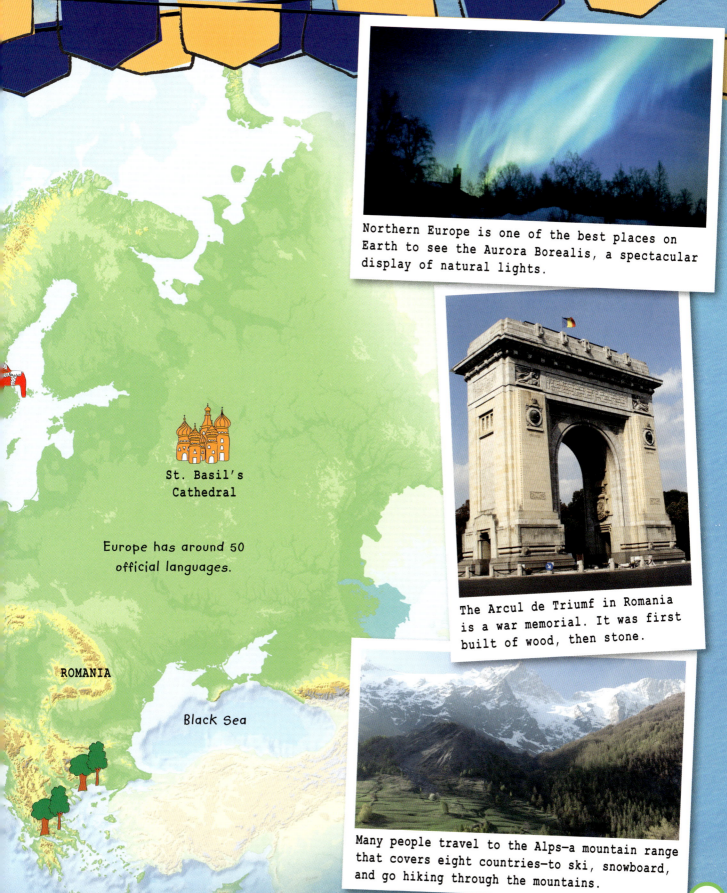

Northern Europe is one of the best places on Earth to see the Aurora Borealis, a spectacular display of natural lights.

St. Basil's Cathedral

Europe has around 50 official languages.

ROMANIA

Black Sea

The Arcul de Triumf in Romania is a war memorial. It was first built of wood, then stone.

Many people travel to the Alps—a mountain range that covers eight countries—to ski, snowboard, and go hiking through the mountains.

Postcards from Asia

Asia is the **BIGGEST** continent and it has the most people by far. It's also one of the most diverse continents.

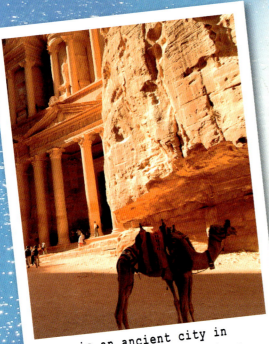

Petra is an ancient city in Jordan. Many of the buildings are carved into the rock.

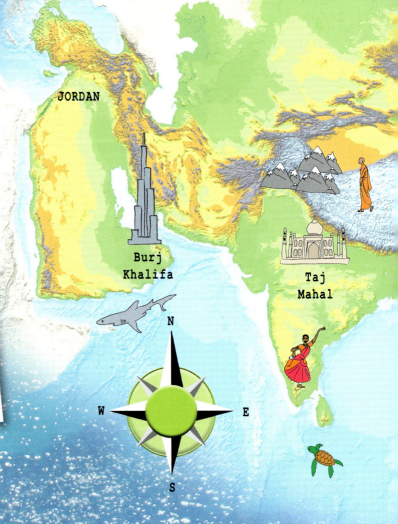

JORDAN

Burj Khalifa

Taj Mahal

N

W   E

S

Most of Russia
is in Asia.

Great Wall
of China

JAPAN

CHINA

Bangkok

Petronas
Towers

Tokyo is the capital city of Japan. On clear
days you can see Mount Fuji from there, even
though it's nearly a hundred miles away.

More than a billion people live in China.
That's more than ALL the people in Europe.
Shanghai is one of China's biggest cities.

Some people travel by water through Bangkok in
Thailand. There are even riverboat markets.

Postcards from Australia

The continent of Australia is made up of the country Australia and a few island countries nearby.

RUGBY is a popular sport ALL OVER Australia.

Most people in Australia live by the coast.

Uluru

Indian Ocean

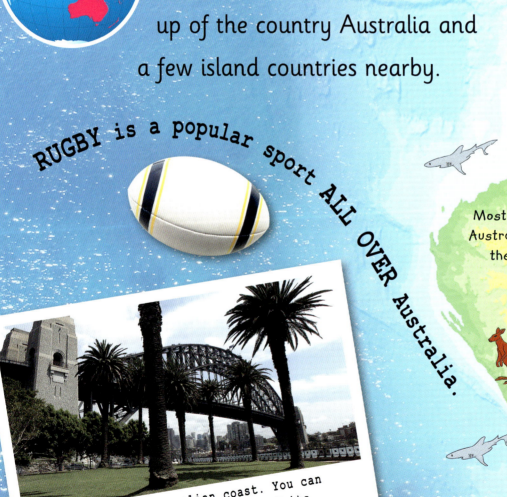

Sydney is on the Australian coast. You can see lots of the city from the top of its famous Harbour Bridge.

Fiji is a country that is made up of more than 330 islands. Around 110 of these have nobody living on them.

This is the largest coral reef in the world.

Great Barrier Reef

New Zealand has two main islands. The North island has geysers that shoot out steam!

AUSTRALIA

Sydney Opera House

New Zealand, Fiji, and many Pacific island countries are not technically on any continent, but we put them together under the name "Australasia."

NEW ZEALAND

N
E
S

Postcards from Antarctica

It's a big **continent** with almost no people or animals. Why not, you ask? Well, it's very, **VERY cold**.

Frozen continent

Antarctica's land is mostly covered in snow and ice. At REALLY cold times of year, the ocean freezes and the Antarctic gets even bigger.

No one lives on Antarctica all the time.

Antarctica is where you'll find the South Pole.

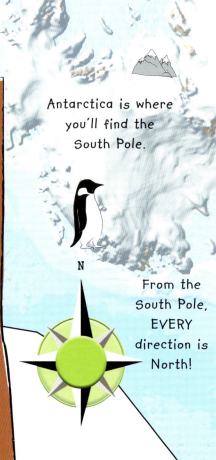

North Pole this way

From the South Pole, EVERY direction is North!

Where's the Arctic?

The Arctic (where the North Pole is), is at the other end of the Earth. It's made of ice and a lot of animals live there, but it isn't a continent.

The people who come here are usually scientists. They use special cars to study and travel across the frozen land.

Emperor Penguins have thick feathers that keep them warm on the Antarctic ice.

The South Pole

It almost never rains in Antarctica. That means it's a very cold desert!

Most of the world's supply of fresh water is frozen in the ice caps of Antarctica.

Very important things about

animals

Animals are the wonderful creatures that share our planet. They include beautiful birds, fantastic fish, marvelous mammals, and so much more. Animals come in all shapes, sizes, and colors, from a **BIG** blue whale, to a **teeny tiny** insect.

What are **animals?**

All plants and animals are living things. What makes animals special is they choose to move around and must eat to survive.

Mammals

If an animal feeds its babies with **milk**, it's a mammal. Most of them have **fur**, but they can all look very different.

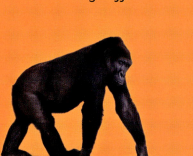

Gorilla

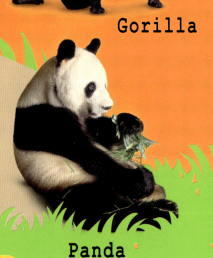

Panda

Birds

Our **feathered friends** are birds. All birds have feathers, but not all of them can **fly**. Some of them can swim and run fast though.

Kingfisher

Flamingo

Reptiles

These **scaly** creatures are **cold-blooded**. This doesn't mean their blood is cold, it means they need the sun to heat up their bodies.

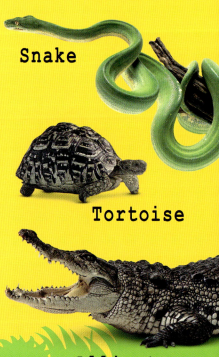

Snake

Tortoise

Alligator

Type trouble?

Animals come in all shapes and sizes! To make it easier, every animal belongs to a **group**.

What about ME?

You're a mammal like us!

Amphibians

Most amphibians are born in **water** and go through big changes as they grow up. As adults they can live in water or on land.

Toad

Frog

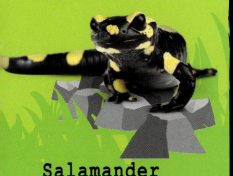

Salamander

Fish

Fins help make fish super swimmers! Fish can be found in oceans, rivers, lakes, ponds, and streams. They breathe in water using **gills**.

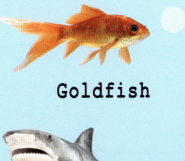

Goldfish

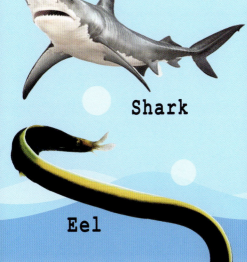

Shark

Eel

Invertebrates

Invertebrates don't have a **backbone**. Most have a shell or a soft body. There are so many different types!

Butterfly

Centipede

Octopus

Dinosaurs once ruled the Earth

Long before people existed, giant reptiles called **dinosaurs** ruled the Earth for millions of years... but where are they now?

The fearsome T. rex had enormous bone-crushing teeth.

Dinosaurs lived in different time periods, so many of the ones on this page **never met**!

Sinosauropteryx
(SIGH-no-sore-OP-ter-ix)

This dinosaur had feathers but it couldn't fly.

Tyrannosaurus rex
(TIE-ran-oh-SORE-us)

Triceratops means "three-horned face."

Triceratops
(try-SERRA-tops)

End of an era

About 66 million years ago, a massive **meteorite** hit the Earth and caused a huge dust cloud that blocked the sun's light. Without it, the dinosaurs couldn't survive.

Why do all of our names have to be so difficult to spell?!

Therizinosaurus
(THERRY-zin-oh-SORE-us)

Mamenchisaurus
(ma-MEN-chee-SORE-us)

Spiky plates

Stegosaurus
(STEG-oh-SORE-us)

Velociraptor
(vel-OSS-ee-RAP-tor)

Don't I look scary? I have feathers, jaws, and razor-sharp claws.

Winged wonder

In 2015 Chinese scientists discovered the remains of a dinosaur called **Zhenyuanlong suni**. It's the biggest winged dinosaur ever discovered, and a relative of the famous Velociraptor.

Mighty mammals

These clever creatures come in all **shapes** and **sizes**, from the mini mouse to the long-necked giraffe. You're a mammal too—all people are!

This sea giant may look like a big fish, but all whales are mammals.

Mother's milk

Mammals can seem very different to each other—and they are! But one thing they all have in common is that mammal moms make milk to feed their babies.

Whale

✓ Babies drink milk

✓ Most are furry

✓ Most don't lay eggs

✓ Warm-blooded

I'm your relative! Monkeys, apes, and humans belong to a group called primates.

Bats come out at night to find food.

Bat

Monkey and baby

We are the only mammals that really fly. Other mammals, such as giant flying squirrels, only glide rather than fly.

Elephants use their trunk like a hand.

Elephant

Bear

Quack quack?
Despite its bill and webbed feet, this is actually a platypus, not a fuzzy duck. It is one of the only mammals that lays eggs.

Tiger and cub

Gorilla

Fabulous fish

From giant sharks to tiny sea horses, fish can look very different from one another. But all fish are perfectly suited to **life in water**.

Sharks are fish too!

Goldfish are popular pets, sharks are not!

Fins help fish stay upright.

Fishy facts

Rather than breathing with lungs, fish breathe using their gills. And unlike mammals and birds, most fish are **cold-blooded**. This means they can't warm their own bodies.

- ✔ Many have scales
- ✔ Breathe with gills
- ✔ Cold-blooded
- ✔ Have fins

Flying fish

Stingray

Sharks and rays have cartilage—a tough, flexible material that makes up their skeleton.

Catfish

Pufferfish

Moray eel

I swim by wiggling my tail fin from side to side.

Sea horse

Tang

There are more than 30,000 different species of fish.

Clownfish

It's sea horse dads, not moms, that give birth to their babies.

Beautiful **birds**

Look up! It's easy to spot a **bird**. Some may fly, some may talk, others may swim, others may squawk. Birds are the only animals with **feathers**.

Birds don't have teeth in their beaks.

Toucan

- ✓ Have feathers
- ✓ Lay eggs
- ✓ Have beaks
- ✓ Warm-blooded

Fantastic feathers

No matter where a bird may live, its feathers keep it dry and warm. And without their feathers, birds wouldn't be able to fly!

Eagle

We are the smallest birds in the world. Our eggs are TINY.

Hummingbirds

Macaw

Woodpecker

Pelican

Ostrich and chick

I'm so big that I can't fly, but I'd rather run fast than be up in the sky.

Chicken

Flightless birds

Try as they might, some birds, such as penguins and ostriches, **can't fly**. But ostriches can run very fast, and penguins are really good swimmers.

Ducks

Scaly reptiles

Whether they slither, scurry, snap, or hiss, all reptiles have scales. Like a suit of armor, scaly skin protects them from predators. It is also waterproof.

Hot and cold

Reptiles are cold-blooded. This means their body doesn't naturally help to cool them when they are hot, or warm them when they are cold.

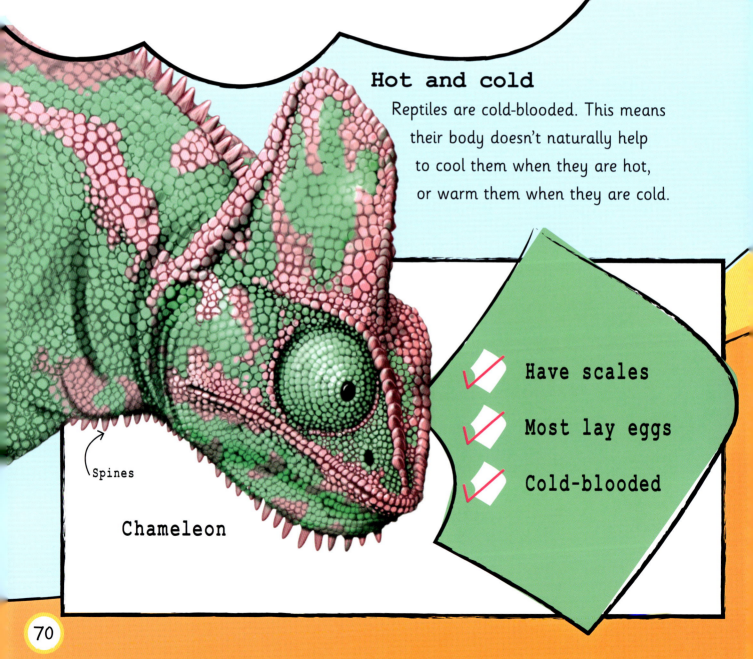

Spines

Chameleon

✓ Have scales

✓ Most lay eggs

✓ Cold-blooded

Frilled lizard

Don't make me angry! If you do, I will open my frill and hiss to scare you away.

Snake

Snakes shed a layer of skin when it gets too tight. This is called molting.

Crocodile

Tuatara

A group of tortoises is called a creep.

Tortoise

Collared lizard

I mostly eat insects, but if I'm very hungry, I might eat other small lizards!

Geckos have sticky feet for climbing.

Geckos

Awesome amphibians

These animals have **super powers**.

Well, not really, but they can live on both **land** and **water**. That's pretty super!

Life cycles

Frogs, like most amphibians, are born from eggs. They slowly grow and change in the water until they are ready for life on land.

Frog

Eggs

Froglet

Tadpoles

Poison
dart
frog

 Moist skin

 Cold-blooded

 No hair or fur

 Can live on land or water

Color caution

A lot of the brightest and most colorful frogs are **poisonous**. It's very clever—their colors are a way of warning "**don't eat me!**"

Teeny tiny frog!

I'm a salamander. My body and tail are very smooth and slimy.

Axolotl

Toad

Salamander

Say my name like "AXE-oh-LOT-el"

Caecilian

Frog

Brilliant bugs

Think of a place. **Any** place in the world...
Bugs live there! There are lots of types
of bug. Which ones do you know?

Munch!
Munch!

Ladybug

Gold
beetle

Feelers

Green
shield bug

Beautiful beetles

There are more types of beetle in the
world than of any other animal. There
are probably lots more to **discover**.

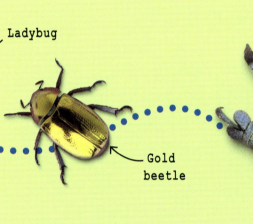

✔ **Three body
sections**

✔ **Many have
wings**

✔ **Six legs**

Wings

= Insect
A beetle is an **insect**.

Fly

Wicked webs

Most spiders spin **webs** to catch their food. Spiders usually eat insects such as flies, but very big spiders can catch birds.

Two body sections

✓ Eight legs

✓ Two body sections

✓ No wings

= Arachnid
A spider is an **arachnid.**

Eight legs

Snail trail

Garden snails like to come out at night to nibble on plants. Wherever they go, they make a trail of **slime** to move along smoothly. How slick!

✓ One body section

✓ One long foot

✓ No legs

Shell

One body section

= Gastropod
A snail is a **gastropod.**

One long foot

Caterpillar to butterfly

What's that? Caterpillars turn into beautiful **butterflies**? How does that happen?

2

A **caterpillar** hatches from an egg.

Pupa

3

The caterpillar grows up and changes into a **pupa** (or a chrysalis).

1

A butterfly lays **eggs** on a leaf.

Egg

The layers of a butterfly's wings are so thin you can actually **see through** them.

Monarch butterfly

The monarch butterfly can live up to nine months.

4

After a while the pupa opens and out comes a **butterfly**!

Empty pupa case

Stretching out

Butterfly **wings** are folded and wrinkly at first, but they soon **stretch out** so the butterfly can fly away.

Animal habitats

Every animal has a special place that they call **home**. In the animal world we call these places habitats.

Forests

More than **half** of the world's animal and plant species live in rain forests!

It's important to look after our habitats.

I love living in the forest! I'm a great climber, and I use my tail to balance.

Oceans and seas

Salty oceans and seas are brimming with fish, mammals, and other sea creatures.

Deserts

Not that many animals can live in a desert because there isn't much **water** to drink.

Rivers and lakes

Lakes and rivers have **fresh water**, which means it isn't salty.

Grasslands

Food can be hard to find in grasslands, especially during the **dry season**.

Pole to pole

It's very cold near the **North** and **South Poles**.
But that doesn't some stop animals from living there!

North

South

These Arctic animals see almost **no daylight** in winter and almost **no darkness** during summer.

Reindeer

Walrus

Snowy owl

North Pole
(The Arctic)

Polar bears

Underneath my fur, my skin is black!

Seals

A polar bear's fur helps it blend in with the snow.

Penguin domination

There aren't very many types of animal in Antarctica, but millions of penguins love it!

Emperor penguins

Fur seal

My favorite food is yummy fish.

King penguins balance their egg on their feet to keep it warm.

I fly between both poles!

Arctic tern

King penguins

I'm one of the smallest types of penguin.

Adélie penguin

South Pole (The Antarctic)

I spy... on the farm

From sheep and cows to goats and horses, there are lots of animals to spot at a **farm**. Which ones can you see?

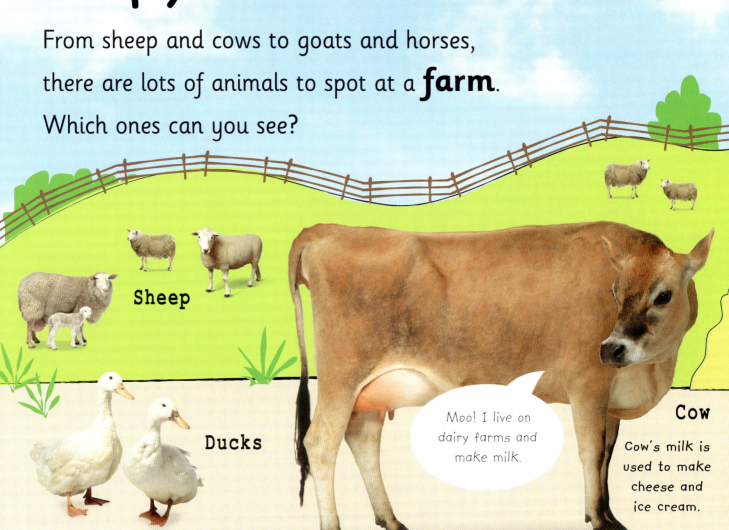

Sheep

Ducks

Moo! I live on dairy farms and make milk.

Cow

Cow's milk is used to make cheese and ice cream.

There are farms that have just one type of

Growing crops

A lot of farmland is used to grow crops. This is where most of our food comes from. The most common crops are corn, rice, and wheat.

Corn

Also known as maize, corn is a popular food to eat. There are lots of corn farms in the USA.

A rooster sings "cock-a-doodle-do!"

Chickens

I help out by carrying people on my back.

Horse

Turkey

Goat

Farm tasks

Farms help us get the things we need, such as eggs for our breakfast and wool for our clothes.

Pig

Pigs love to roll in mud, but not because they're dirty—the mud stops them from getting sunburned!

animal, such as salmon or even snails!

Rice

Delicious rice needs lots of water to grow. In parts of Asia, people eat rice almost every day.

RICE

Wheat

Wheat is used to make lots of foods, including bread, pasta, and cakes!

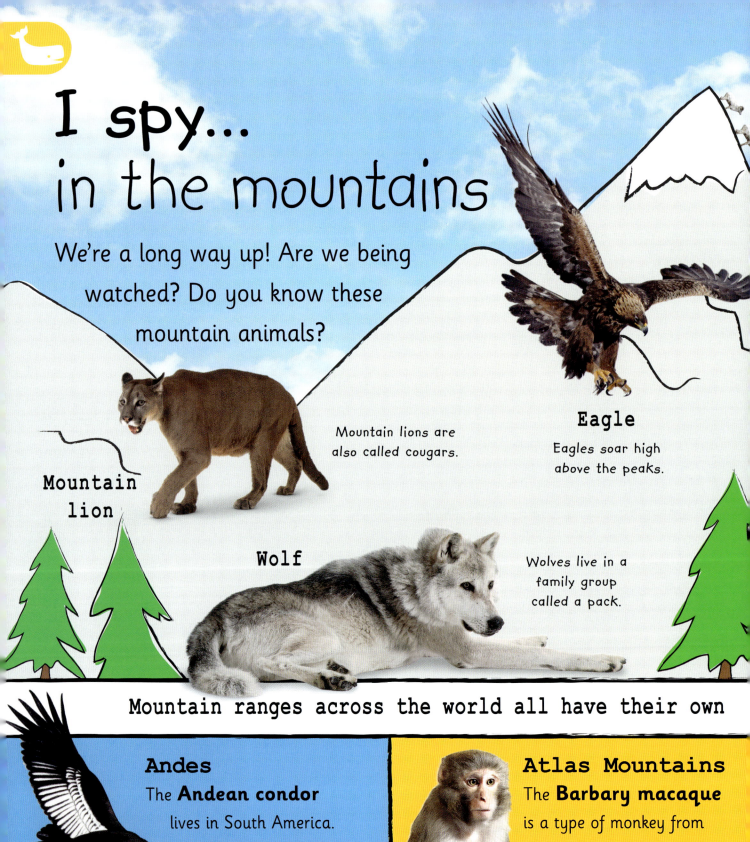

I spy...
in the mountains

We're a long way up! Are we being watched? Do you know these mountain animals?

Mountain lion

Mountain lions are also called cougars.

Eagle

Eagles soar high above the peaks.

Wolf

Wolves live in a family group called a pack.

Mountain ranges across the world all have their own

Andes
The **Andean condor** lives in South America. Its huge wings help it glide through the air.

Atlas Mountains
The **Barbary macaque** is a type of monkey from Africa. The leaders of each group are always female.

Coyotes love to howl at the Moon.

Black bears are very good at climbing trees.

Black bear

Coyote

Mountain goat

I'm an amazing climber. You should see me walking on cliffs.

special animals. Here are some you may not know.

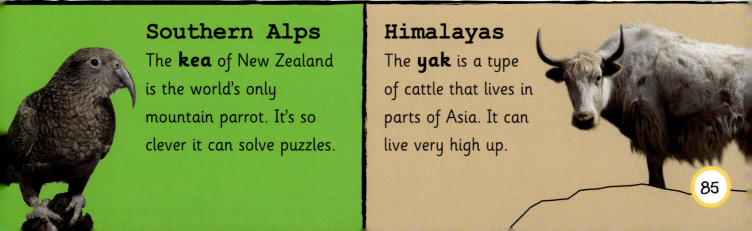

Southern Alps

The **kea** of New Zealand is the world's only mountain parrot. It's so clever it can solve puzzles.

Himalayas

The **yak** is a type of cattle that lives in parts of Asia. It can live very high up.

Desert animals

Hot and **dry** deserts aren't as empty as they look. Some animals are perfectly adapted to live there.

I'm on lookout duty! I stand up tall to spot dangers and protect my family.

Meerkats live in big family groups called mobs.

Meerkats

Camel

A camel's hump is full of fat!

I can go for weeks without any water!

Thirsty weather

Animals need to drink, but there isn't much **water** in the desert. All these animals have adapted to only drink every now and then.

Diadem snake

Spiny mouse

Thorny devil

This lizard lives in the Australian Outback.

Desert scorpion

I spy...
on the African plains

Let's go on a **SAFARI**! There are so many exciting animals to see on the African plains.

Giraffes

A giraffe's long neck helps it reach leaves high up in the tree tops.

Gazelles

Zebras

While the African grasslands are hot and dry, they also

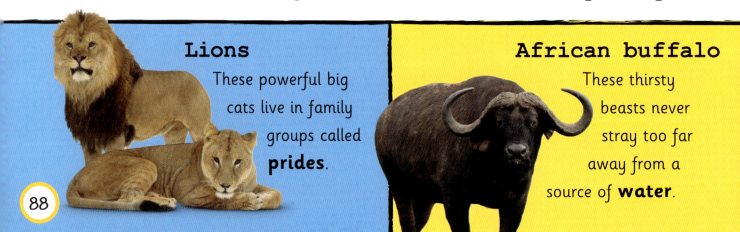

Lions
These powerful big cats live in family groups called **prides**.

African buffalo
These thirsty beasts never stray too far away from a source of **water**.

Where's the water?

The African plains are wide, open grasslands. It's hot and dry there, so animals gather around **watering holes** to drink.

I like to climb trees. Sometimes I bring my meals up here, too!

Leopard

Elephants

African elephants are the biggest land animals in the world.

Hippopotamus

have a rainy season that helps plants grow.

Leopard

Quick and agile, a leopard's coat helps it to **hide** in grass while it is hunting.

White rhino

Although this two-horned animal looks like a slow, **heavy giant**, it can actually run very **fast**.

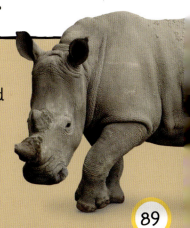

The very big blue whale

A giant of the sea, there's no creature anywhere that's the size of the big **blue whale**.

Barnacle

I'm big. VERY big!

A blue whale's heart is as big as a car.

Even longer than a BUS.

Mighty mammal

Whales aren't fish (like sharks), so they have to come up to breathe air. They are **mammals**, like mice, but **SO MUCH** bigger!

Blue whales are bigger than even the biggest dinosaurs!

I'm a tiny barnacle and clinging is my thing, I eat the whale's leftovers and live like a King.

Enormous mouth

Blue whales aren't just big, they're LOUD! Whales can make sounds as loud as an AIRPLANE taking off.

Big appetite

A blue whale's food is teeny tiny itsy bitsy **krill**. To fill up, the whale has to eat 40 million a day. That's **LOADS!**

Krill

Super sharks

They may look all toothy and scary, but guess what—a lot of sharks are **harmless**.

What are sharks?

Sharks are a type of fish. They swim in every sea and some rivers. Most sharks have lots of teeth, but others have none.

I'm the GREAT WHITE shark, the deadliest hunter in the ocean!

Great white shark

Sharp teeth

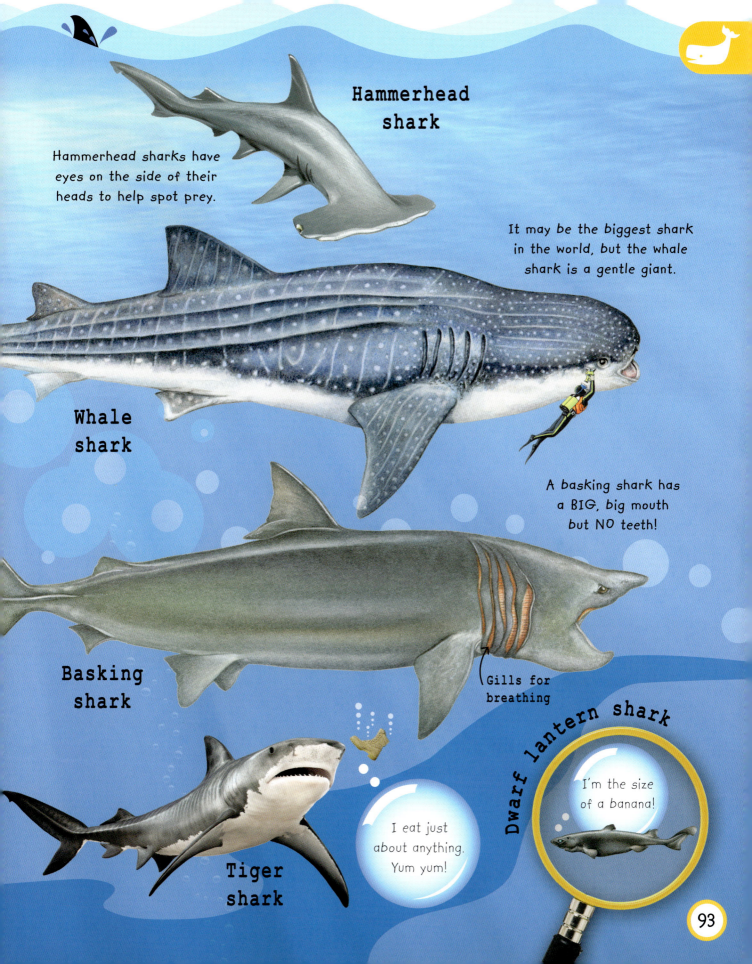

Hammerhead shark

Hammerhead sharks have eyes on the side of their heads to help spot prey.

It may be the biggest shark in the world, but the whale shark is a gentle giant.

Whale shark

A basking shark has a BIG, big mouth but NO teeth!

Basking shark

Gills for breathing

Dwarf lantern shark

I'm the size of a banana!

Tiger shark

I eat just about anything. Yum yum!

Primate party

These clever, curious, and chatty creatures are part of an animal group called **primates**.

Monkeying around

If someone calls you a silly monkey, it's almost true! Humans are closely related to **chimps**, who are very smart apes (but not monkeys).

Chimpanzee

Orangutan

Orangutans love to eat fruit.

People are primates too!

Swing kings

Some primates, like monkeys, have **tails**, but chimpanzees and gorillas (which are both apes) do not.

Capuchin monkey

Monkeys can use their long tails to climb trees.

I live on the forest floor with my gorilla pals. I'm too big and heavy to live up in the trees.

Howler monkey

Cover your EARS! Howler monkeys are VERY NOISY.

Spider monkey

Gorilla

Sloths aren't lazy! We just take our time.

Speedy species

How fast can you run? Check out the competition in the animal kingdom with these very **fast**, and very **slow**, animals.

START

Sea horse
Sea horses are very slow swimmers.

Human

Wait for me!

Snail

Ostrich

Dolphin

Dolphins can jump high out of the water.

Ostriches may not be able to fly but they can run very fast!

Strong swimmers

Polar bears can swim fast and cover huge distances. Scientists tracked a bear who swam for **nine days** without stopping to eat or sleep.

I dive to catch my prey.

Peregrine falcons can dive faster than any other animal can move!

FINISH

Horse

Alpine swift
Alpine swifts fly very quickly, and they hardly ever stop to perch or land.

Cheetah

Cheetahs are the fastest land animal.

Look how quick I am!

Horse-fly

Look at me swim!

Sailfish

Big cats

Have you seen pet cats relaxing, purring, chasing, and playing? Well big cats do that too!

Hard to spot

Some big cats have **patterned fur** to keep them hidden when hunting.

Leopard

Cheetahs can run very fast! Don't let the yawn fool you.

Cheetah

Most big cats are the top

Tiger

Tigers are the **biggest** and **strongest** of all the big cats.

Domestic cat

If you watch your pet cat, you'll see some **similarities** with the big cats!

Purr-fect hunters

Big cats are **carnivores**. This means they eat meat, and have to hunt for their dinner.

Lions live in family groups called prides.

Lions

Female lionesses look after the cubs and do most of the hunting.

hunter in their environment.

Black panther

Panthers are really black leopards, but it's hard to see their **spots**.

Snow leopard

Snow leopards have very **thick fur** to keep them warm on cold mountains.

Animals after dark

While you sleep at night, a secret world is **waking up**.

Meet the curious creatures that come out after dark.

We call these animals **nocturnal**.

My long nose helps me to sniff out food.

Armadillos have long tongues for catching ants.

Badger

Aardvark

Armadillo

Smell and hearing, touch and sight,

Fennec fox

The smallest fox is called the fennec fox. It lives in hot, dry deserts and uses its big ears to **listen** for prey.

Raccoon

Using an incredible sense of **touch**, raccoons can feel their way around in total darkness.

I fly so quietly that my prey never hears me coming.

Owl

Bat

I have great hearing.

Right for night

Nocturnal animals have special nighttime powers like great **eyesight** or super **hearing** that help them in the dark.

Play-fighting helps fox cubs learn how to hunt.

Foxes

Hedgehog

Wolf

Wolves have super night vision—all the better to see you with!

help these creatures feed at night!

Kiwi

Kiwis live in New Zealand. They can't fly or see very well, but they have nostrils at the tip of their beaks to **sniff** out food.

Bush baby

These little creatures are found in Africa. They have big eyes that help them **see**.

The **tortoise** and the **hare**

There once was a **very fast hare** who loved to boast about his **super speed**.

Start

One day, a wise old **tortoise** challenged the hare to a **race**.

Nearly there!

zzzzZZ

With the tortoise so far behind, the hare decided to stop for a relaxing **nap** under a tree.

He's making a mistake!

Because tortoises are **slow**, the hare thought he would win **easily**.

Go, go, go!

The hare sped away like a flash, while the tortoise plodded along **slowly and steadily**.

Halfway

As the hare slept, the tortoise caught up and walked past him on his way to the **finish line**.

Finish line

The tortoise was **proud** that he didn't give up, and the hare felt **silly** for being so careless.

1st

Very important things about

people

The way we live today is all thanks to the people who have **created** and **discovered** wonderful things. We've come a long way since humans were making cave paintings. Now we can cure lots of diseases, travel around the world, and even go to the moon!

Very early humans

A lot of what we know about **early people**, we learned from things they made and their cave paintings.

Early people would have had to live near water, so lots of cave paintings show rivers and streams.

Saber-toothed tiger

How did they do it?
Some drawings were scratched into rocks, but others were made with a kind of paint made from **animal fat** and charcoal.

Mammoths don't exist today. They were like bigger, hairier elephants.

Lots of cave paintings show pictures of animals that lived at the time.

Mammoth

Clever clues

We don't know much about early humans, so their cave paintings give us helpful clues.

Hunting tools

Woolly rhino

Early discoveries

These discoveries seem so simple to us now, but they were all so important that it's impossible to imagine our world without them.

We first made fires by rubbing sticks together.

Fire

Learning how to make fire meant we could **cook** our food. Over time, this changed our brains and bodies, which allowed us to become smart enough to invent and discover other things.

Fire was (and still is) a very important source of heat and light.

The wheel

We still use wheels to get around and move **heavy** objects, but before the wheel was invented we could only push heavy things or roll them over logs!

Ancient stone wheel

This is VERY heavy!

Without wheels, we wouldn't have cars or bikes.

Tools

All sorts of jobs, such as hunting, making clothes, and farming the land, became much easier when we started making and using tools.

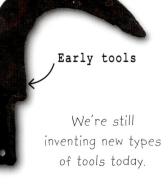

Early tools

We're still inventing new types of tools today.

The time of the pharaohs

A long, long time ago powerful people called **pharaohs** ruled over the advanced ancient civilization of **Egypt**.

Mummy mystery

When a pharaoh died he was made into a **mummy** and buried in a fancy box called a sarcophagus (sar-COFF-a-guss).

This is the sarcophagus of the pharaoh Tutankhamun (toot-en-car-moon).

Then and now

Even though they lived so long ago, the ancient Egyptians did a lot of things that we do today.

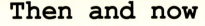

THEY WORE MAKEUP
Everyone wore eyeliner.

THEY WROTE THINGS DOWN
Their writing even had pictures.

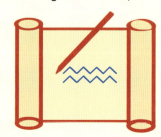

Mummies were wrapped up in bandages before they were buried.

The tallest building in the ancient world was the Great Pyramid at Giza. It still stands today.

Ancient Egyptians found ways to transport stone over long distances and build the **pyramids**. These massive monuments were tombs for pharaohs.

Meow!

THEY WORE SOCKS
Yes, really!

THEY CLEANED THEIR TEETH
The Egyptians even invented a type of breath mint!

THEY HAD CATS
Cats were seen as very important. Some were made into mummies.

Ancient China

During the country's **long** history, Chinese people have built, discovered, and invented many important things.

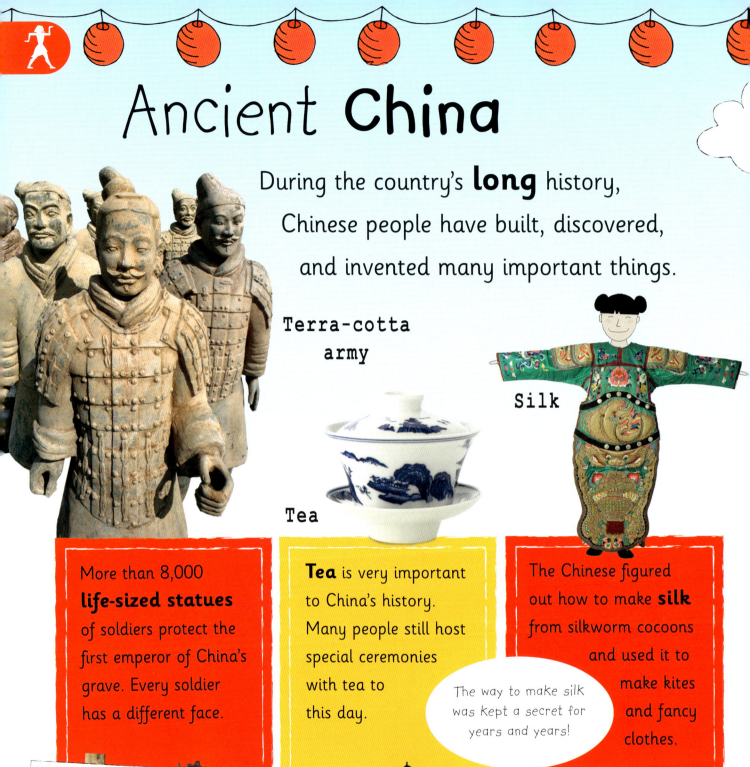

Terra-cotta army

Tea

Silk

More than 8,000 **life-sized statues** of soldiers protect the first emperor of China's grave. Every soldier has a different face.

Tea is very important to China's history. Many people still host special ceremonies with tea to this day.

The Chinese figured out how to make **silk** from silkworm cocoons and used it to make kites and fancy clothes.

The way to make silk was kept a secret for years and years!

The Great Wall of China.

Gunpowder, paper, printing, and the compass are often called China's Four Great Inventions.

Compass

Kite

Gunpowder is what makes fireworks go BANG!

The **compass** was a Chinese invention that helped sailors and explorers find their way at sea.

More than just a fun toy, Chinese people used **kites** to test the speed of the wind and send signals to each other.

There aren't many things more important than **paper**. Without paper, you couldn't read this book!

中国

The Chinese use symbols, not letters.

First Australians

The First Australians lived in Australia **long before** anyone else, and they still live there today. Their way of life has continued for thousands of years.

Uluru

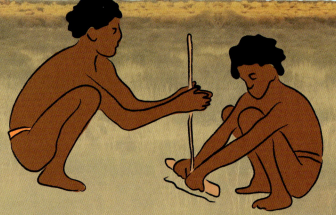
In the past, sticks were used to make fire.

Spiritual people

All First Australians feel connected to the **land**. They have many beliefs, stories, and legends about how the world was created.

Many First Australians tell tales about the world through

Signs and symbols

First Australian art uses symbols to tell stories. This is what a few of the symbols mean.

Human footprint

River

Boomerangs are sticks that come back when you throw them.

A sacred rock

Uluru is a massive rock that is very important to First Australians. At the bottom, there are caves filled with ancient paintings.

The didgeridoo is an anceint musical instrument that is still played today.

MUSIC, DANCE, STORIES, and ART.

People around campfire

Kangaroo tracks

Water hole

Really modern Romans

The **ancient Romans** were a group of people who lived long ago. But much of their lives were really quite modern.

Water ways

The Romans invented **aqueducts**. These special bridges carried water to towns and cities.

Big baths

Most Romans didn't have baths at home. They went to public baths and had to wash with their friends.

We Romans loved big feasts.

Now and then

The Romans were really clever. They used or invented a lot of things that we still have today!

They figured out how to blow into hot glass to make goblets.

They had toilets and sewers!

When it erupted, Mount Vesuvius destroyed the city of Pompeii and covered it in ash.

Roman chariot

Romans went to stadiums, like the Colosseum in Rome, to watch shows. The Colosseum still stands today!

Romans enjoyed watching gladiator fights. Sometimes, gladiators even fought lions!

The Romans built long, straight roads.

"I came, I saw, I conquered."

Julius Caesar, a Roman general, once said this. Caesar wanted to expand Rome, so he conquered many lands.

They were the first people to use concrete for building.

They had police and fire fighters!

Viking raiders

Coming from Scandinavia (that's Norway, Denmark, and Sweden), the Vikings were the fierce warriors, raiders, traders, and invaders of old Europe.

Super ships

Viking longships could travel in deep or shallow water. This allowed the Vikings to travel up rivers for sneak attacks.

Mighty warriors

Brilliant at **surprise attacks**, Vikings were very fearsome fighters who took lots of weapons and armor into battle.

Sharp axes and spears were sometimes thrown at their enemies.

Viking swords were very strong and sharp on both edges.

Powerful people

The Vikings believed in the Norse gods.
They include **Odin**, the god of war,
Freyja, the goddess of love,
and **Thor**, the god of thunder.

Many people think Vikings had
horns on their helmets, but
they didn't! It would have been
too easy to knock them off!

Viking shields were made of
wood and had an iron center
which protected the hand.

Ancient Americans

From farmers and builders to warriors and thinkers, many different ancient civilizations once called Central and South America home.

What links them?

Although these people lived in different places at different times, farming **maize** was very important to their ways of life. They also built many great temples and statues, and worshipped lots of gods.

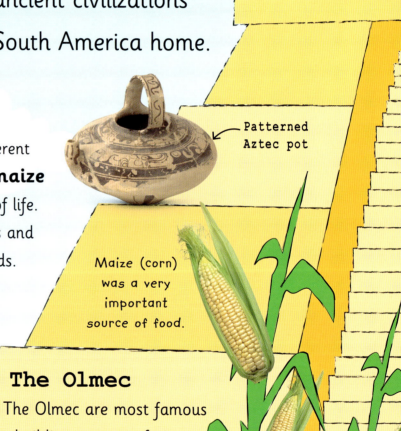

Patterned Aztec pot

Maize (corn) was a very important source of food.

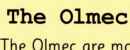

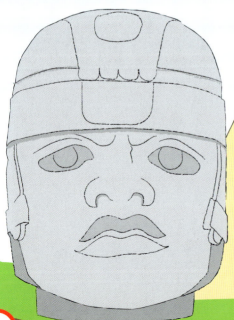

The Olmec

The Olmec are most famous for building statues of giant heads. Many people think the Olmec influenced both the Maya and Aztec way of life.

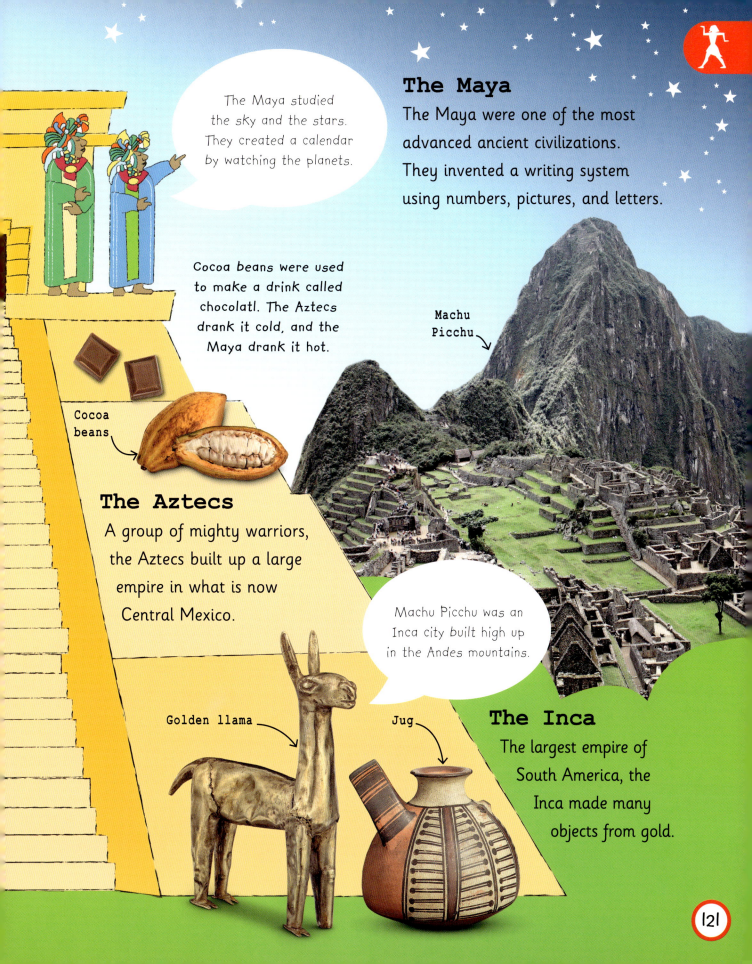

The Maya studied the sky and the stars. They created a calendar by watching the planets.

The Maya
The Maya were one of the most advanced ancient civilizations. They invented a writing system using numbers, pictures, and letters.

Cocoa beans were used to make a drink called chocolatl. The Aztecs drank it cold, and the Maya drank it hot.

Machu Picchu

Cocoa beans

The Aztecs
A group of mighty warriors, the Aztecs built up a large empire in what is now Central Mexico.

Machu Picchu was an Inca city built high up in the Andes mountains.

Golden llama

Jug

The Inca
The largest empire of South America, the Inca made many objects from gold.

Indigenous peoples

Long before Europeans arrived in the America, there were already many groups of people living all over North America.

Where were they?

Different tribes and communities lived all over the continent. Some lived in the Plains and slept in tents called tipis.

Totem poles are built to show important things, such as family history, people, or events.

Some tribes believed a dance could bring rain to help crops grow.

Totem pole

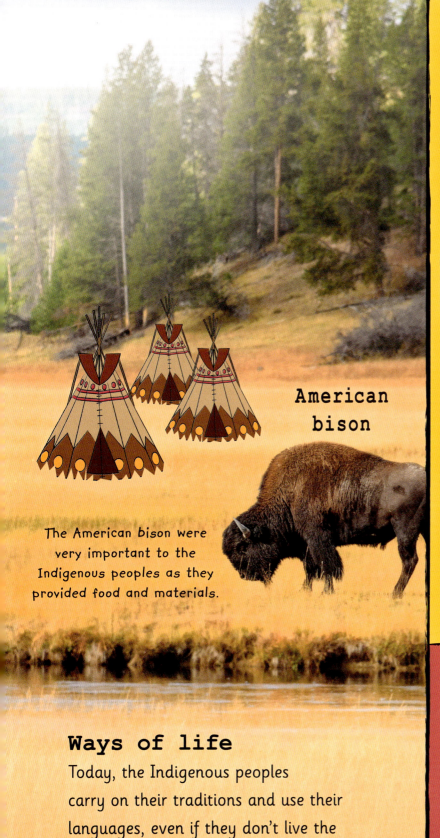

American bison

The American bison were very important to the Indigenous peoples as they provided food and materials.

Ways of life

Today, the Indigenous peoples carry on their traditions and use their languages, even if they don't live the same lifestyle as their ancestors.

Special items

The Indigenous peoples invented many things, including activities like lacrosse and tobogganing.

Eagle feathers

This war shield was used by the Taos Pueblo people.

The most respected warriors of the Sioux people wore special war headdresses.

Ceremonial tomahawk

The tomahawk was a type of ax used as a tool or a weapon.

Corn (maize) was a very important crop and source of food.

Festivals and celebrations

Old or new, big or small, **festivals** are a great way for people to come together and celebrate!

January

New Year's Day celebrates the beginning of the year—often with fireworks.

February

Groundhog Day is a tradition in the US to celebrate that spring is on its way.

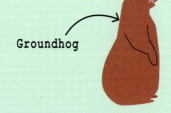

Groundhog

March

For **Hinamatsuri**, Japanese people display dolls to wish young girls happiness and health.

Traditional doll

July

The **Mud Festival** in South Korea is all about mud, and how great it is!

August

Awa Odori is a traditional Japanese street dance festival.

September

South African people celebrate their culture on **Heritage Day**, with big feasts.

Diwali

The festival of **lights** is a time where people pray for good fortune.

Lunar New Year

A very important Asian holiday that invites good luck.

Passover

A Jewish holiday that remembers **Moses** with a meal called "seder."

Eid al-Fitr

A festival that marks the end of the holy month of **Ramadan** for Muslims.

April

Songkran is a New Year's celebration in Southeast Asia where people have water fights!

May

Cinco de Mayo remembers a Mexican victory with parades, dancing, and food.

June

The Andean people hold **Inti Raymi**, the Incan Sun Festival, on the shortest day of the year.

October

During **Halloween**, children dress up in scary costumes and eat candy.

November

Dia de los Muertos remembers those who have died through food and decorations.

December

Christmas is a Christian holiday that celebrates the birth of Jesus.

Eager explorers

Over the centuries, many **travelers** have journeyed across the world, exchanging information, inventions, and a variety of foods.

Food staples, such as **corn**, potatoes, tomatoes, and cassava were sent across the world from the Americas.

Christopher Columbus

Columbus was searching for a faster way to travel to Asia from Europe, but instead he reached the **Americas**.

Gertrude Bell

I learned eight languages so that I could speak to the people I met on my travels.

Gertrude Bell explored the history and cultures of the **Middle East**. She was also a spy for the British during World War I!

Marco Polo

Marco Polo spent 24 years traveling around **Asia**. He returned to Europe and told people about lots of Chinese inventions.

Ibn Battuta

Zheng He

After spending most of his life traveling around Africa, Asia, and the Middle East, Battuta wrote a **book** about his journey.

The Chinese explorer Zheng He led more than 300 ships on **seven expeditions** to explore Asia and Africa.

Important inventors

These **brain boxes** are just some of the clever inventors whose ideas helped change our world.

Paper

Printing press

Computer program

Before **Cai Lun** invented **paper**, people had to make do with writing and drawing on cave walls, silk, or even bone!

Cai Lun used squashed up plants to make paper.

Without **Johannes Gutenberg**, you would not be reading this book! His **printing press** allowed people to share their ideas and stories.

Ada Lovelace wrote the first program for early computers. She also got people thinking about all the complex things computers could do.

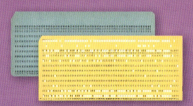

Lovelace suggested using punched cards as a way to input data in a computer.

World wide web

Light bulb

3-D illusion

Thomas Edison's

brightest idea was to create a new and improved **light bulb**. If it wasn't for his work, you might be reading this book by candlelight!

Edison invented hundreds of things during his lifetime.

Tim Berners-Lee

had a very clever plan for computers all over the world to be able to communicate. This is known as the **World Wide Web.**

Valerie Thomas's

innovation is the reason that we enjoy 3-D graphics today. She invented a way to **transmit three-dimensional images** so they look real.

Super scientists

Scientists help us understand our world. So without these clever people, we'd know **much less** than we do!

Zero

Planets

Soil improvement

Aryabhatta was a mathematician and astronomer. He is best known for coming up with the **concept of zero**.

Galileo Galilei was a genius who invented a new **telescope** and showed that heavier items don't fall quicker than lighter ones.

George Washington Carver, an agricultural scientist, developed ways to improve the **soil** and crop cultivation through his scientific research.

Galileo was the one to discover that Jupiter has moons!

Galileo found out a lot about the universe.

$$E = mc^2$$

Radiation

Energy

Space

Marie Curie was a science whiz who experimented with **radioactivity**. She won the Nobel Prize, an award given to scientists, TWICE!

Albert Einstein is known for his scientific work and theories, including an equation that is used to calculate **energy**.

Einstein's brain was studied by scientists to see what made him so smart.

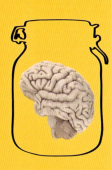

Katherine Johnson's knowledge of math and computers helped NASA send successful missions, like Apollo 11, into space.

Travel by land

Have you ever noticed how many different vehicles there are on the road? There are tons!

Cool cars

You can go far and fast in a car. Some people race fast cars for fun.

Car

Bicycle

Road trips

Vehicles help us move people or objects from one place to another **much quicker** than by walking. Do you recognize any of these?

Farmers use tractors to help them on the farm.

Tractor

Motorcycle

Train

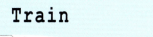

Trains travel quickly across the land. The **Shanghai Maglev Train** is the fastest in the world. Blink and you'll miss it!

Camper **Truck** **Taxi**

Taxis take people where they want to go.

Big rig

Taxis in NEW YORK are yellow.

Dump truck

Fire engine

Emergency vehicles make loud noises to tell other drivers they are nearby.

To the sea

Travel by **water**

Our world is full of water, from oceans and rivers, to canals and lakes. **Boats** allow us to move across them.

Cruise
ship

Ocean motion

Boats move across the water in different ways. Most boats are powered by engines, but others rely on the **wind**.

Cruise ships are like water hotels. They're so huge they have restaurants, swimming pools, and even tennis courts!

Fishing boat

Rowing boat

Speedboat

Container ships move **HEAVY** things across the sea.

Container ship
Boats are better than planes for carrying heavy items, since they're bigger and stronger.

Sailing boat

These boats move when strong winds blow their sails.

Jet Ski

Tug boat

Little tug boats are strong enough to tow much **BIGGER** ships.

Junk boat

Hovercraft

Hovercrafts have a big cushion that lets them travel on water or on land.

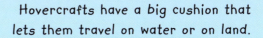

Travel by **air**

Let's take a journey into the sky. Is that a big mechanical bird? No, it's a **plane**! Soaring high and moving fast, where's it off to today?

Glider
PH-308

Airplane

Biplane

Biplanes are one of the oldest types of plane, but pilots still fly them today.

Cockpit

Landing wheels

Stairs

Speedy travel

Airplanes are the fastest way to get across the world. Before planes, people had to rely on boats, which are much slower.

Propeller

Light aircraft

G-AYFC

Smart pilots

People who fly aircraft are
called pilots. It takes a lot of
practice and skill to be a pilot.

Hot-air balloon

Tail →

← Wing

↑
Engine

Baggage
truck
↘

Helicopter

These planes fight each other in the sky.

Fighter jet

Fighter jets fly so
quickly they can travel
faster than sound!

Totally tall towers

Modern buildings reach up so high in the sky it looks like they go up forever. It's no wonder we call them **skyscrapers**!

Taipei 101
1,670 ft
(509 m)

Petronas Towers
1,483 ft
(452 m)

Empire State Building
1,453 ft (443 m)

Eiffel Tower
1,063 ft
(324 m)

Shard
1,017 ft
(310 m)

How do I get down from here?

Right now clever architects are coming up

Amazing places

Buildings don't have to be tall to be well-known. Here are some other famous buildings from around the world.

Angkor Wat

Leaning Tower of Pisa

It leans because it's too heavy for the soft ground that it's built on.

Brilliant builders

The people who design buildings are known as **architects**.
It's a job that takes lots of hard work and planning.

Burj Khalifa
2,716 ft
(828 m)

Shanghai Tower
2,073 ft
(632 m)

Tokyo Skytree
2,080 ft
(634 m)

Lotte World Tower
1,821 ft
(555 m)

The Burj Khalifa has been the world's tallest building since it opened in 2010.

with ways to build even taller buildings!

Taj Mahal
This beautiful monument in India is the tomb of an emperor's wife.

The Forbidden City

Emperors of China lived in this palace for hundreds of years.

I want to be an **astronaut!**

Do you think you've got what it takes to be a space explorer? Hold onto your seat! **3...2...1... LIFT OFF!**

Animals were also sent to space.

Living in space

Being an astronaut is **hard**! Life in space is different to life on Earth in lots of ways. Such as:

🚀 Food is specially prepared by scientists on Earth so that it lasts a long time.

🚀 Toilets are different to the ones on Earth. They work a little like a vacuum cleaner!

🚀 There's no "day" or "night" in space, so astronauts have to keep to a strict sleep routine.

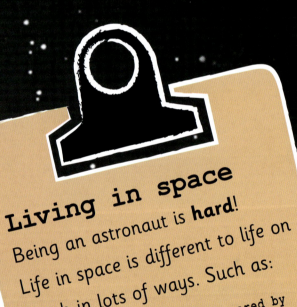

Astronauts are strapped in when they sleep so they don't float away!

Even busy astronauts get free time to enjoy themselves.

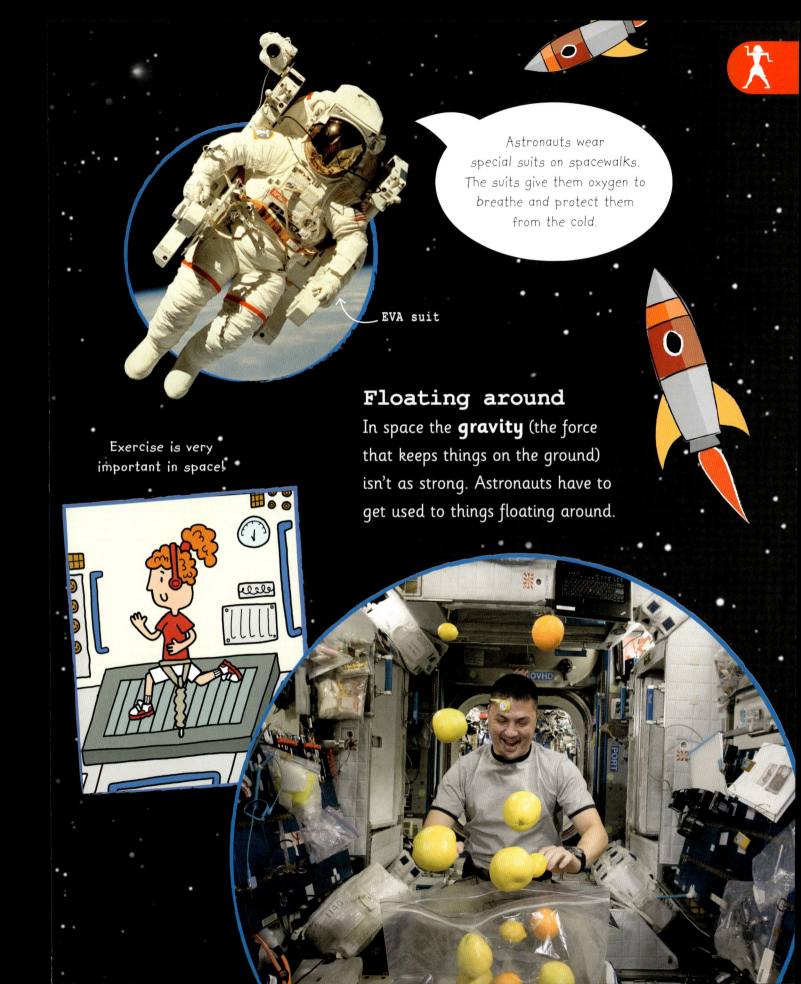

Astronauts wear special suits on spacewalks. The suits give them oxygen to breathe and protect them from the cold.

EVA suit

Exercise is very important in space!

Floating around

In space the **gravity** (the force that keeps things on the ground) isn't as strong. Astronauts have to get used to things floating around.

Flying to the moon

IIn the year 1969, three brave astronauts became the first people to **land on the moon**. This important mission was called **Apollo 11**.

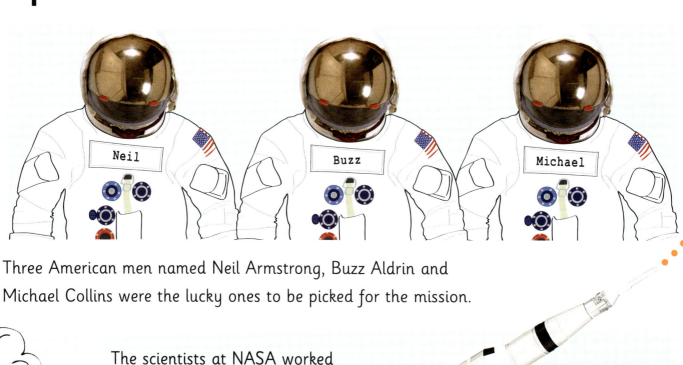

Neil

Buzz

Michael

Three American men named Neil Armstrong, Buzz Aldrin and Michael Collins were the lucky ones to be picked for the mission.

The scientists at NASA worked very hard to make sure the launch went smoothly and **safely**.

The rocket blasted off from a place called Cape Kennedy, Florida in July 1969.

It took more than three days to get to the moon.

The spaceship traveled through space to get to the moon. During this time the astronauts did experiments and **sent messages** to the scientists on Earth.

"That's ONE SMALL STEP for man; one GIANT LEAP for mankind."

Finally they reached the moon! Two of the three astronauts, Armstrong and Aldrin, landed on the surface in a small vehicle called "The Eagle." Armstrong climbed down a ladder and walked on the surface.

Meanwhile... More than 500 MILLION people across the world watched the moon landing on their televisions.

Very important things about

me

Right now, you're using **more** than your eyes to read this book. Your brain is working hard to help you see these words and get them to make sense. Your body is an amazing **machine**, and this section is all about **YOU** and the important things in your life.

The human body

Your body is an amazing machine! Inside it are lots of parts that all work together.

Skeleton

Your skeleton is made up of lots of **bones**. It's what keeps your body's shape.

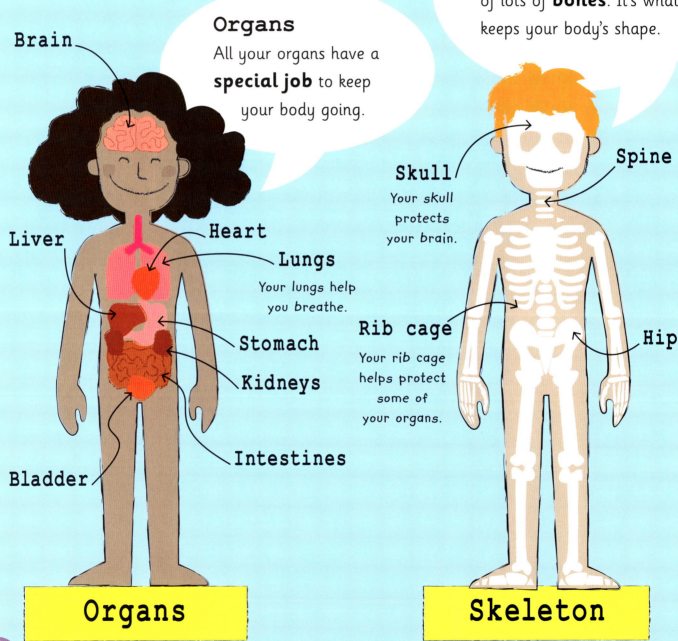

Organs

All your organs have a **special job** to keep your body going.

Brain

Liver

Heart

Lungs

Your lungs help you breathe.

Stomach

Kidneys

Intestines

Bladder

Skull

Your skull protects your brain.

Spine

Rib cage

Your rib cage helps protect some of your organs.

Hip

Organs

Skeleton

Muscles

Your muscles let you **move**. You need them to run, jump, smile, lift objects, and more!

Skin

Your skin wraps around your body to keep it **safe**. It's also your body's biggest organ.

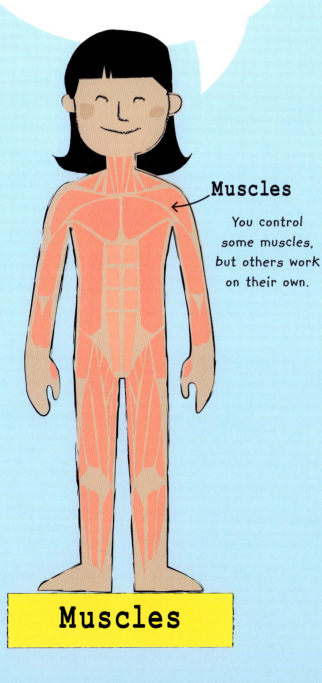

Muscles

You control some muscles, but others work on their own.

Muscles

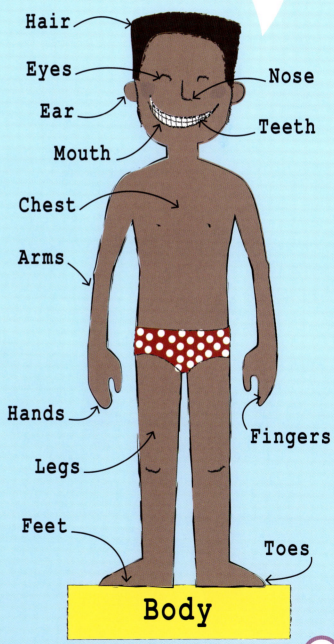

Hair
Eyes
Ear
Mouth
Chest
Arms
Nose
Teeth
Hands
Legs
Feet
Fingers
Toes

Body

My blood

Everybody needs oxygen to live. You get oxygen when you breathe, and your blood **takes it** around your body.

What is blood?

Blood is a mixture of a liquid called plasma and lots and lots of teeny tiny things called "cells."

Blood travels quickly through tubes called blood vessels.

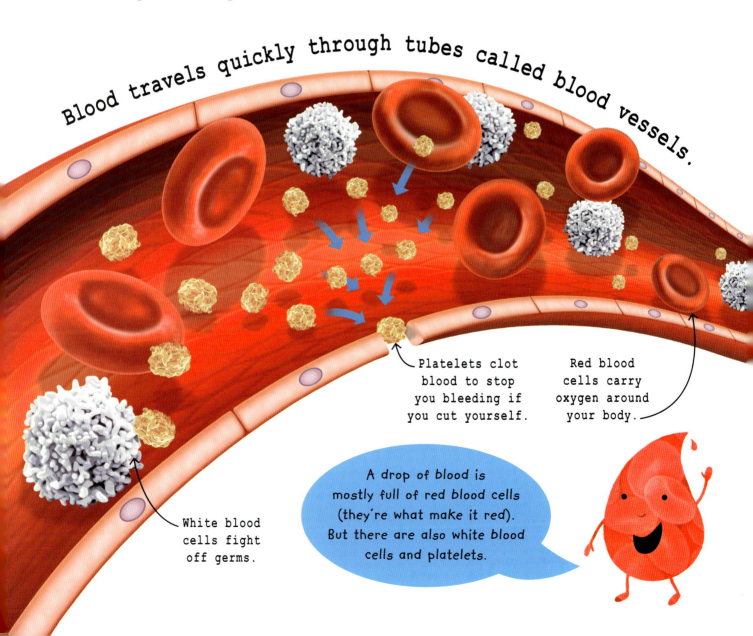

Platelets clot blood to stop you bleeding if you cut yourself.

Red blood cells carry oxygen around your body.

White blood cells fight off germs.

A drop of blood is mostly full of red blood cells (they're what make it red). But there are also white blood cells and platelets.

Your **HEART** pumps blood around your body. Up to the top of your **HEAD**, and down to the tips of your **TOES**.

A blood cell travels around the body in 60 seconds!

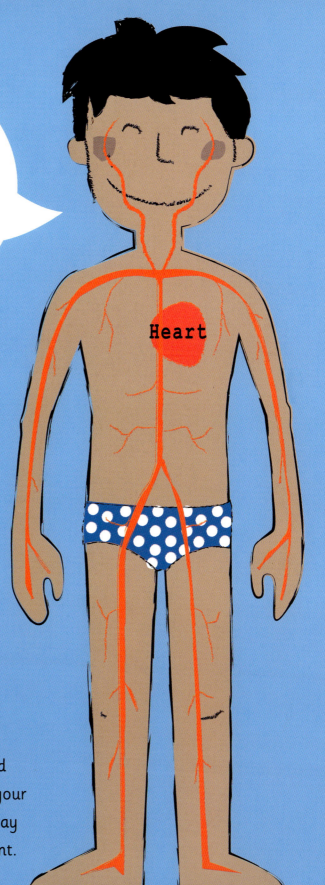

Heart

Clever cleaning

As well as delivering oxygen and other important things around your body, blood also helps takes away waste that the body doesn't want.

Sense-ational

Sometimes the world can be confusing! But the five main **senses** work together with our brain to help us understand and interact with it.

Touching

Smelling

Seeing

Hearing

Tasting

You can **touch** and feel things using your hands (or any part of your body, really).

Feathers feel soft, but you wouldn't want to touch a spiky cactus.

Your nose picks up **smells** (both nice and nasty ones!) Without smell you wouldn't be able to taste much either.

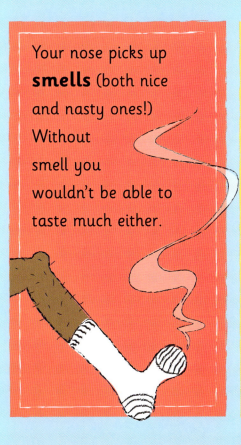

Both of your eyes work together to help you to **see** the world in front of you and find your way around.

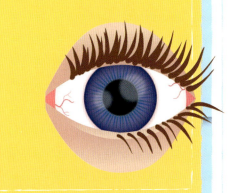

Experts say the feelings we get when we're hungry, thirsty, or itchy, may be **other senses**. Here are a few more:

It's not nice to feel pain, but it's your body's way of letting you know that something is wrong.

Our sense of balance keeps us upright and stops us falling down.

Have you noticed you can feel if something is hot or cold without touching it?

Shh! Your ears let you **hear** noises. They never stop listening, even when you sleep!

The smallest bone in your body is found in your ear.

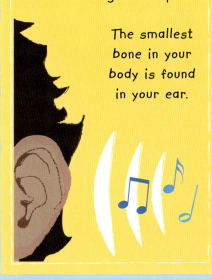

The tongue has teeny tiny taste buds that let us **taste** the flavors in our food.

salty

sweet

Sour

Your brain uses more ENERGY than any other body part.

Sharing work

Because the brain has **SO** much to do, the different parts all works together, even when you are asleep.

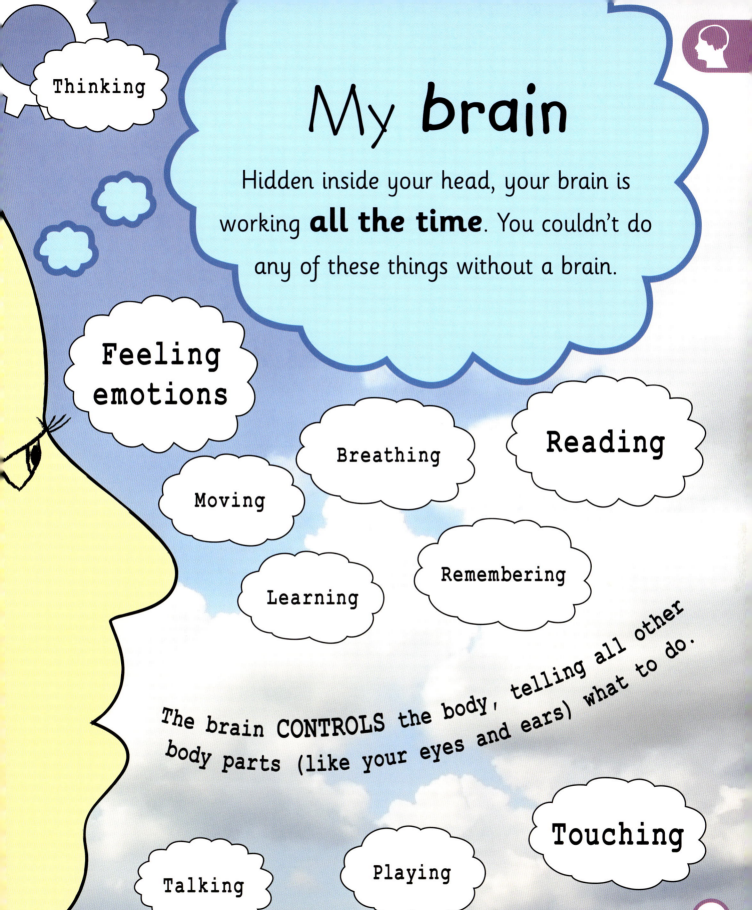

Thinking

My **brain**

Hidden inside your head, your brain is working **all the time**. You couldn't do any of these things without a brain.

Feeling emotions

Breathing

Reading

Moving

Remembering

Learning

The brain CONTROLS the body, telling all other body parts (like your eyes and ears) what to do.

Touching

Talking

Playing

Sleep time

When you close your eyes and need to **rest**, sleep is just the very **best**!

How much sleep do we need?

Although they sleep A LOT, babies wake up between naps.

Babies
Most of the time!

Almost everyone has dreams while they sleep

Sleepy animals
Many animals have unusual or surprising sleeping habits.

Some mammals, such as **hedgehogs**, hibernate. This means they sleep all through winter.

The **swift** is a very fast bird that can sleep while it flies!

Why do we need sleep?

Sleep helps our body heal, grow, and stay healthy. It also gives us energy so we can be active throughout the day.

Rest and a good bedtime routine is important for a growing child.

Teenagers need lots of energy to grow into their adult bodies.

The older you get, the less sleep you will need.

**Children
10-12 hours**

**Teenagers
8-10 hours**

**Adults
6-8 hours**

but they don't always remember them.

Cute **koalas** love to slumber. They sleep around 18 hours a day.

Giraffes don't need much sleep at all. They usually sleep standing up!

Good **food**

Food makes us feel full, happy, and healthy (if we eat the good stuff!) Let's chew, munch, and chomp.

Pasta

There are lots of shapes of pasta.

Pineapple is very sweet and juicy.

Peas

Pineapple

Fruit
The super cool **heroes** of the food world, fruits are packed with all the goodies that help keep you healthy.

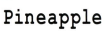

Vegetables
Always try to **eat your greens** (and other colored veggies). They make your meals tastier and healthier.

Carbs
Pasta, rice, potatoes, and bread are all foods that give you lots of **energy** to run around and play.

"Carbs" is short for "carbohydrates."

INSECTS are eaten by a BILLION people across the world.

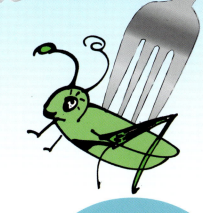

Eggs help to make your muscles strong.

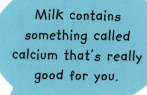

Milk contains something called calcium that's really good for you.

Milk

Cupcake

Egg

Protein

Foods high in protein, such as beans, nuts, eggs, and meat help your body **repair** itself and help you to grow.

Dairy

A great way to keep your teeth and bones healthy is by eating dairy—foods that are made from **milk**.

Cheese, butter, and yogurt are made from milk.

Sweets

Eating too many fatty or sugary foods can be unhealthy. But there's nothing wrong with an occasional **treat**!

Let's communicate

Telling other people what you think and how you feel is important, so it's a good thing there are lots of different ways to do this.

A wave can mean hello or goodbye.

We all speak and think in a language (there are more than 6,000 in the world!). Some people can speak lots of different languages.

Talking is one of the ways that people can communicate with each other.

You don't always need words. People can often work out how you feel by the look on your face.

You can sometimes tell how a person is feeling by the way they act or their body language.

Some people communicate by making signs with their hands. This helps if you're speaking to someone who can't hear well.

Wonderful writing

Reading and writing is another way to communicate. Languages can be written in different alphabets or scripts, so they don't always look the same.

All these words mean "HELLO."

Hello
English

नमस्ते
Hindi

السلام علیکم
Arabic, Persian, and Urdu

你好
Mandarin

Hello! How are you?

Brilliant braille

Braille is a written language that uses raised dots for letters. It helps people who can't see well to read with their fingers, not their eyes.

Hello in braille

Emoji

In digital messages, we can show how we feel with icons and pictures as well as words.

Marvelous music

There are lots of different types and styles of **music**, and almost as many ways for us to **enjoy** it!

There are lots of musical instruments to play, but it takes **time** and **practice** to become very good.

The **voice** and **mouth** are amazing instruments. They can be used to sing, hum, or whistle!

Music is often written down so you know what note to play next.

Singing

Playing

Interesting instruments

The triangle is simple to learn but hard to master!

Bagpipes are played in Scotland. They are very LOUD!

Although they are huge, harps make a soft sound.

The pipa has been played in China for more than 2,000 years.

Music can **affect** you in many ways. Listening to it can calm you down, cheer you up, or even help you concentrate.

Sometimes, the beat of a tune makes you want to **move** and dance!

People enjoy different forms of music.

Dancing can be a lot of fun!

Listening

Dancing

Amazing art

Whether you paint, draw, take photos, or sculpt, there are so many ways to create beautiful things.

This statue was carved from one piece of marble!

Crafts and collage are fun too!

Painting

With just a brush, some paints, and a little practice, people can create beautiful images on canvas or paper.

Sculpture

Sculptures are a type of 3-D art. They can be made from almost anything—from marble to trash!

Photography

Cameras let you capture a moment in time and see the world from different angles.

Cameras let in light and turn it into pictures.

Drawing

Using pencils, pens, crayons, or even your computer, you can scribble, sketch, and draw.

Mosaics

This ancient type of art is made by sticking small tiles together to form a bigger image.

Getting better

What do we do if we're not feeling well? We can visit doctors and nurses! Their special skills and instruments can make us feel better.

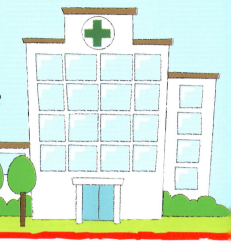

Miraculous medicine

These are some of the developments in medicine that help people to live longer and healthier lives.

Vaccines

A vaccine helps the body fight diseases. Edward Jenner, a British surgeon, created the first successful **smallpox** vaccine.

Stethoscope

The stethoscope lets doctors **listen** to the heart and lungs to see if there are any problems.

Transplant

If someone's heart isn't working very well, they can get a **new one** from a donor.

Thermometer

A high temperature can be a sign of fever. Thermometers help doctors measure **temperature**.

X-rays

Doctors use X-rays to take photos of your teeth and **bones** to see if they are broken.

What is a pandemic?

Some diseases spread between people very quickly, making them sick in large numbers. When such a disease breaks out across the entire world, it is called a pandemic.

During the COVID-19 pandemic, face masks helped people to stay safe from bad germs in public places.

Antibiotics

Antibiotics are very important medicines that are used to fight nasty **infections** in the body.

Casts

A hard cast helps protect broken **bones** and keep them still so they mend and heal properly.

Prosthetic

People who lose an arm or leg, or are born without it are able to have a **prosthetic** (artificial) one fitted.

Surgery

Modern **"keyhole"** surgery is safer than surgery used to be.

Ultrasound

Ultrasounds let doctors look at moving images from inside the body. It's mostly used to check up on unborn **babies**.

Cameras

Endoscope capsules are cameras so small you can swallow them! They let doctors see inside your body.

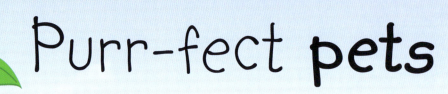

Purr-fect pets

Pets can live in our home or in our yards, and they make great friends. They need lots of **love** and **care**.

Almost half of all households in the USA have a pet dog or cat.

Dogs

Dogs are smart, loving, and loyal. They need daily **walks** and lots of gentle **training**.

Cats

Full of personality, cats make **great company** around the house. They also like to run and play outside. Most of all, they love to snooze!

Birds

Birds need a big **aviary** to live in so that they can fly around. Parrots can live for 90 years, so they are a big **responsibility**!

Fish

A big, clean **tank** with hiding places and other **fishy friends** is important if you want to keep fish.

Chickens

It's best to keep chickens as a group of a few **hens** and one **rooster**. Chickens need space to wander and a nice coop to live in.

Rabbits

Rabbits like to be petted but not picked up. They need rabbit **friends**, lots of **hay**, and a **big home** to run around in.

Fun numbers

Numbers help us to understand the world around us. We mostly use them to count and measure things (and work out when our birthday is!), but some numbers are **really** special.

3, 2, 1…
lift off!

12.30

00   8

0

It may seem like nothing, but try counting, telling the time, or keeping score without **zero**!

3.14

Math experts use "pi" to work out difficult sums. We shorten pi to 3.14 but it's actually **MUCH** longer.

"Pi" sounds like "pie" but you can't eat it!"

4

This number is **unlucky** in some countries where it sounds like their language's word for death.

26

This is the number of **letters** there are in the English alphabet

52

There are 52 **weeks** in a year. That's how long it takes for the Earth to move around the Sun.

60

The number 60 is useful to tell the **time**. There are 60 seconds in a minute, and 60 minutes in an hour.

Inventing numbers

The earliest known number system was developed a long time ago in a place called **Babylonia**. Today numbers are all around us and we use them for all sorts of things.

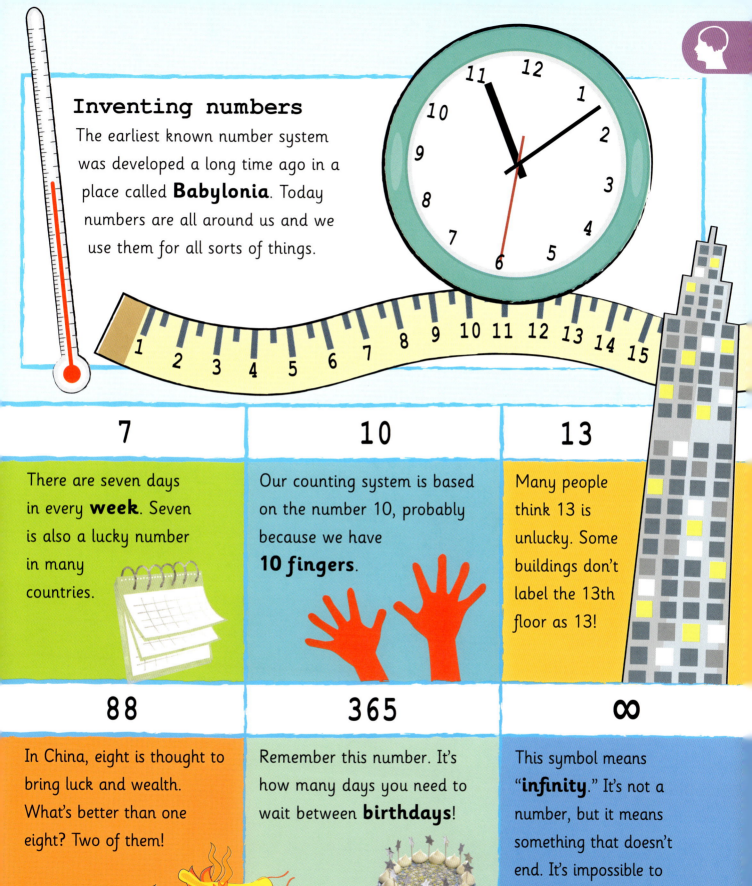

7

There are seven days in every **week**. Seven is also a lucky number in many countries.

10

Our counting system is based on the number 10, probably because we have **10 fingers**.

13

Many people think 13 is unlucky. Some buildings don't label the 13th floor as 13!

88

In China, eight is thought to bring luck and wealth. What's better than one eight? Two of them!

365

Remember this number. It's how many days you need to wait between **birthdays**!

∞

This symbol means "**infinity**." It's not a number, but it means something that doesn't end. It's impossible to count to infinity.

What's the time?

We can't see or feel it, but everything we do takes time. Its most important use is for planning our days. Does this day seem anything like yours?

Wake up, sleepyhead! It's a brand new day.

Breakfast time! You need lots of energy for the day ahead.

It's time for school. What will you learn today?

Is your stomach rumbling? It must be lunchtime!

7am   **7:30am**   **8:30am**   **12pm**

Telling time

We can't feel time, but we can measure it. These numbers help us to do that.

There are **60 seconds** in a **minute**. That's about how long it might take to put on your shoes.

There are **60 minutes** in an **hour**. About the time it takes to eat dinner.

3:30pm

Time to go home. What will you get up to this afternoon?

After-school activities are so much fun!

It's time to sit down and eat your evening meal. Yum!

It's starting to get late. Time to bathe and brush your teeth.

Light's out until tomorrow. Goodnight!

4:30pm　　**6pm**　　**7pm**　　**7:30pm**

A whole **day** (including night) takes **24 hours**. This is how long it takes the Earth to spin around once.

There are **7 days** in a **week**. So it's never too long until the weekend!

The **ant** and the grasshopper

One lovely **spring** day, a grasshopper was playing his guitar, when a little ant walked by...

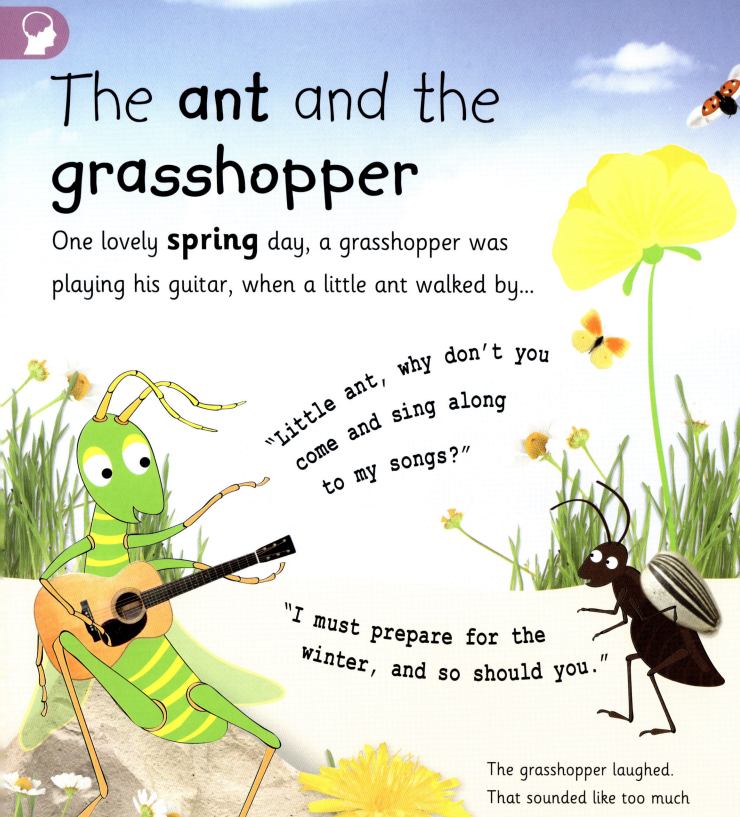

"Little ant, why don't you come and sing along to my songs?"

"I must prepare for the winter, and so should you."

The grasshopper laughed. That sounded like too much work. Besides, winter was such a **long** way away and he had plenty to eat at the moment.

Summer came and went, and the grasshopper continued to laze about. The ant reminded him to **prepare** for winter, but the grasshopper didn't listen.

But winter came earlier than usual that year and the grasshopper was shocked. He was **cold** and **hungry**, and he couldn't find food or shelter anywhere.

"The little ant was right!" he thought sadly. "I must not be so silly next year." Luckily the ant was willing to **share** with him, but the grasshopper learned how important it is to work hard and be prepared.

very important things

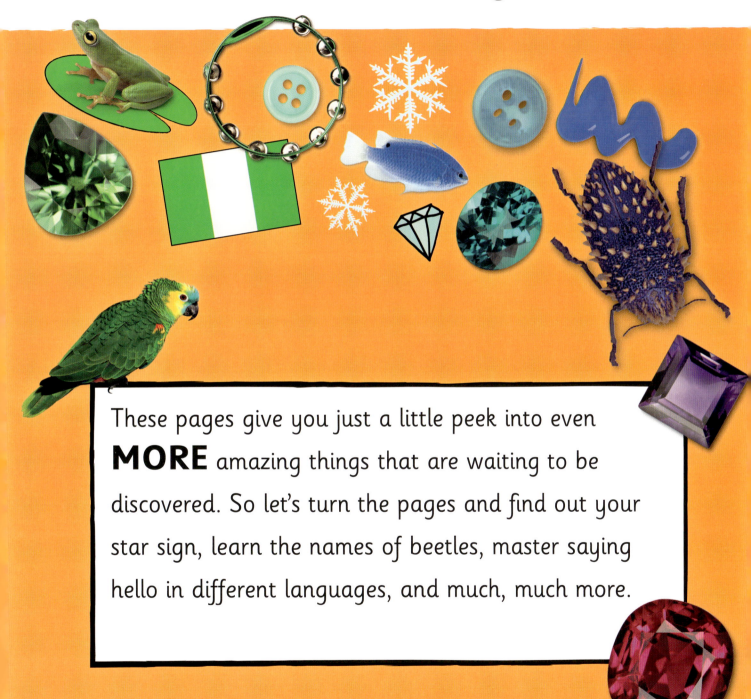

These pages give you just a little peek into even **MORE** amazing things that are waiting to be discovered. So let's turn the pages and find out your star sign, learn the names of beetles, master saying hello in different languages, and much, much more.

Saying hello...

All across the world, people greet each other in different ways. It's good to know how to say **hello**!

English
Hello
(Hell-loh)

French
Bonjour
(bon-zhoor)

Mandarin
Nǐhǎo
(Nee-how)

Portuguese
Olá
(Oh-lah)

Japanese
Konnichiwa
(Kon-nee-chee-wah)

Swedish
Hej
(Hay)

Spanish
Hola
(Oh-lah)

German
Guten Tag
(Goot-en tahk)

Hawaiian
Aloha
(Ah-loh-ha)

Alphabets

Some languages, such as Japanese and Chinese, are written in different scripts or alphabets. So in those countries they'd be written differently to the way you see here.

Dutch
Goed dag
(goot darg)

...and **goodbye**

Now you know hello, this is what the word for **goodbye** looks and sounds like in different languages.

French
Au revoir
(Oh ruhv-wahr)

Mandarin
Zàijiàn
(Zay jee-an)

English
Goodbye
(Good-buy)

Portuguese
Adeus
(A-deh-oos)

Swedish
Hej då
(Hay daw)

Japanese
Sayonara
(Seye-yo-nah-rah)

Spanish
Adiós
(Ah-dee-oss)

German
Auf Wiedersehen
(Owf veed-er-zay-ern)

Hawaiian
Aloha
(Ah-loh-ha)

If you learn other languages you can make friends with people from all over the world!

Dutch
Tot ziens
(Tot zins)

Glorious colors

Our eyes are very special. Thanks to the way they bring in light, we can see a whole rainbow of colors.

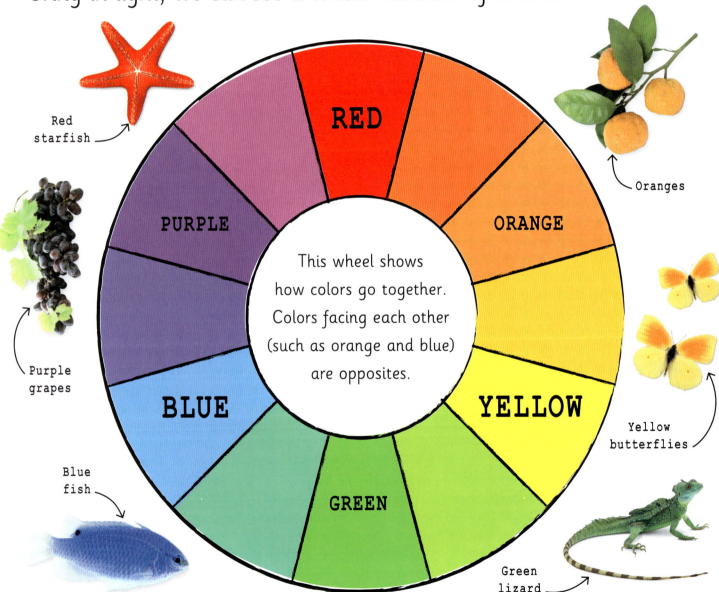

Red starfish

Purple grapes

Blue fish

Oranges

Yellow butterflies

Green lizard

RED

ORANGE

YELLOW

GREEN

BLUE

PURPLE

This wheel shows how colors go together. Colors facing each other (such as orange and blue) are opposites.

Some animals, including DOGS, see FEWER colors than us.

Mix and match

By mixing colors together we can make new ones. Red, yellow, and blue are called **primary colors** because mixing them creates lots of other colors.

Some toucans have colorful bills. Animals may have bright colors to scare off other animals or to attract a mate.

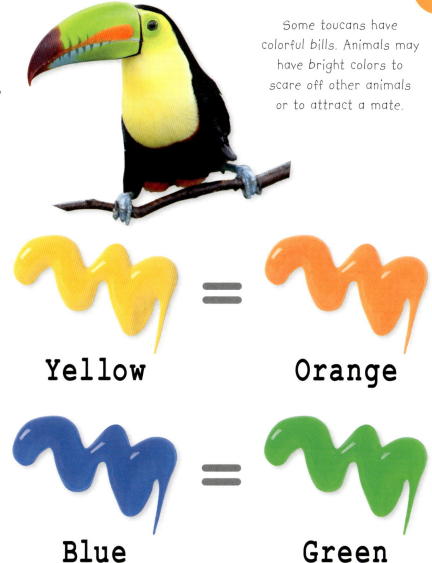

Red + **Yellow** = **Orange**

Yellow + **Blue** = **Green**

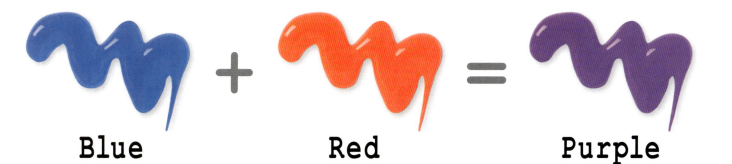

Blue + **Red** = **Purple**

Other animals, such as BUTTERFLIES, can see MORE.

Super shapes

Whether they have pointy edges, twisty curves, or lots of corners, shapes are all around us wherever we go.

2-D shapes are FLAT. You can see the whole shape on paper.

4 equal edges

Square

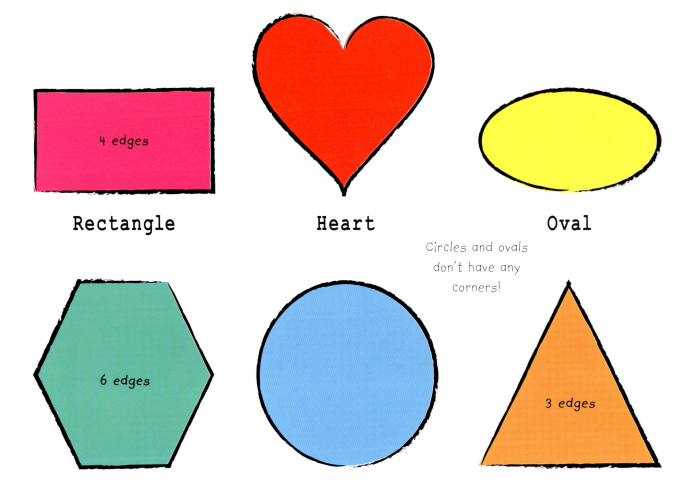

4 edges

Rectangle

Heart

Oval

Circles and ovals don't have any corners!

6 edges

Hexagon

Circle

3 edges

Triangle

These shapes are 3-D. They are the SOLID objects that you can see and touch.

Cone

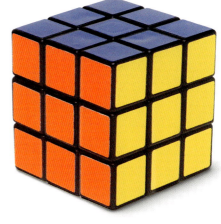

Cube

Cubes and cuboids have 6 faces, but you can't see them all on paper.

Cuboid

Spheroid

Sphere

This pyramid has a square base and four triangles that meet at the top.

Pyramid

Fantastic fruit

Coming in lots of shapes, sizes, and **colors**, all fruits have seeds. Fruits are full of vitamins and minerals, so try to eat some **every** day.

Pineapple

Olives

Avocado

Lemon

Papaya

Grapes

Banana

Watermelon

Kiwi

Starfruit

Apricot

Cherries

Blackberries

Physalis

Apple

Plums

Peach

Hard skin
protects
the fruit

Lychees

Figs

Clementines

Strawberries

Blueberries

Vibrant veggies

Chomping on **vegetables**, whether they're raw or cooked, is a great way of staying healthy. Try to eat them with every main meal.

Ginger

Lettuce

Broccoli

Garlic

Celery

Potatoes

Peas

Zucchini

Asparagus

Cauliflower

Carrots

Radish

Kohlrabi

Carrots aren't just orange. They can be purple too!

Sweet potatoes

Beetroot

Red cabbage

Bell Pepper

Chiles

Red onion

Let's count

1 One elephant

2 Two giraffes

3 Three penguins

4 Four ponies

5 Five mandrills

6 Six parrots

7 Seven tortoises

8 Eight starfish

9 Nine butterflies

10 Ten rabbits

20 Twenty fish

30 Thirty frogs

50 Fifty
ladybugs

We've got lots of spots!

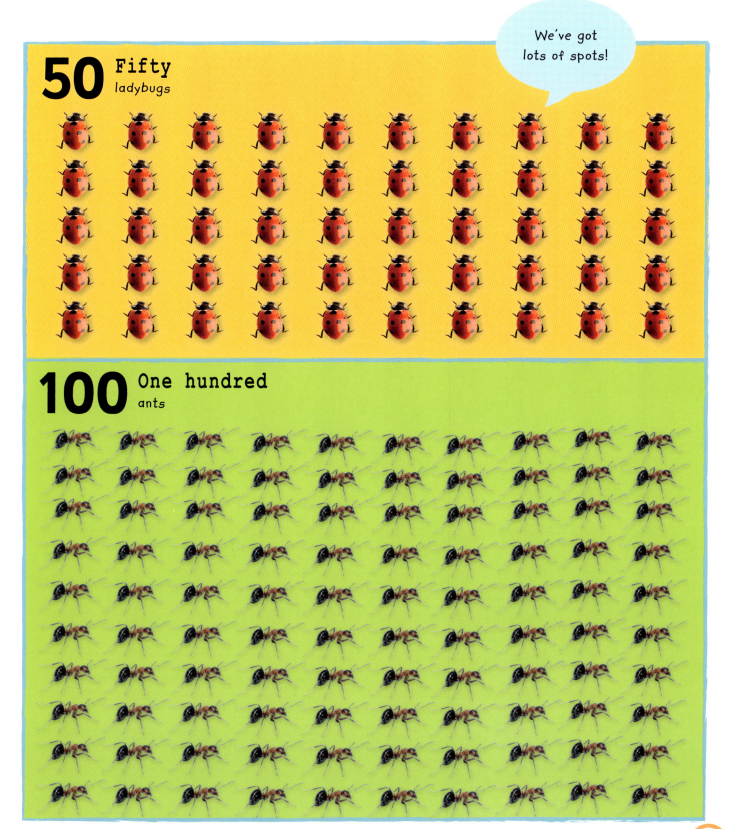

100 One hundred
ants

Let's multiply

Adding up lots of the same number is much **easier** and **quicker** when you use multiplication.

Say you have 4 lots of 2 buttons, that's...

Count them and see for yourself!

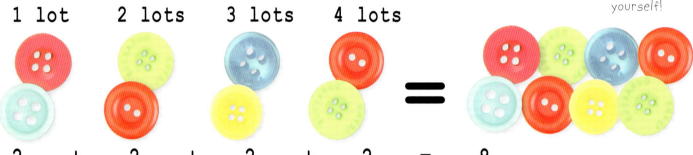

1 lot	2 lots	3 lots	4 lots

2 + 2 + 2 + 2 = 8

$$4 \times 2 = 8 \text{ buttons}$$

Now try finding the answer for these sums using the table.

Using the grid

For "2 x 3", put a finger on the big number "2" and slide it along the line until your finger lines up with the big number "3". Where they meet (6) is your answer!

2 x 3 = ?
8 x 9 = ?
4 x 6 = ?
7 x 5 = ?

It doesn't matter what order you do it in, the result will be the same.

Cheat sheet

This handy table lets you see what two numbers become when multiplied together without having to work it out.

The numbers in white are numbers multiplied by themself!

	1	2	3	4	5	6	7	8	9	10
1	1	2	3	4	5	6	7	8	9	10
2	2	4	6	8	10	12	14	16	18	20
3	3	6	9	12	15	18	21	24	27	30
4	4	8	12	16	20	24	28	32	36	40
5	5	10	15	20	25	30	35	40	45	50
6	6	12	18	24	30	36	42	48	54	60
7	7	14	21	28	35	42	49	56	63	70
8	8	16	24	32	40	48	56	64	72	80
9	9	18	27	36	45	54	63	72	81	90
10	10	20	30	40	50	60	70	80	90	100

Measurements

Figuring things out, from how tall we are to how fast we can run, wouldn't be possible without using measurements.

120cm — 4ft
110cm
100cm
90cm — 3ft
80cm
70cm
60cm — 2ft
50cm
40cm
30cm — 1ft
20cm
10cm

In some countries you would say I am 120cm tall, but in others you would say I'm 4 feet tall!

Measuring size

Metric
Millimeters (mm)
Centimeters (cm)
Meters (m)
Kilometers (km)

Imperial
Inches (in)
Feet (ft)
Yards (yd)
Miles (mi)

Measuring weight

Metric
Milligrams (mg)
Grams (g)
Kilograms (kg)

Imperial
Ounces (oz)
Pounds (lb)
Tons (T)

Other measures
Certain things have a special measurement that's only used for them.

The spicy heat of chili peppers is measured in **scovilles**.

Computer memory is measured with a system called **bytes**.

Measuring methods

There are different ways to measure the same thing depending on where you live in the world. Some countries use a system called "**metric**" and others use one called "**imperial**."

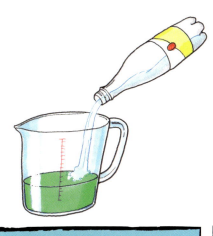

Thermometers help us to measure heat.

Kph and mph are worked out by seeing how far something can travel in an hour.

Measuring liquid	Measuring heat	Measuring speed
Metric Milliliters (ml) Liters (l) Kiloliters (kl)	**Metric** Celsius (°C)	**Metric** Kilometers per hour (Kph)
Imperial Fluid ounces (fl oz) Cups (c) Pints (pt) Gallons (gal)	**Imperial** Fahrenheit (°F)	**Imperial** Miles per hour (mph)

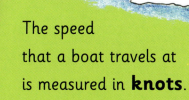

You use **hands** to work out how tall a horse is.

The speed that a boat travels at is measured in **knots**.

Star signs

Every person has a **star sign** with a special symbol. Your sign depends on where the sun was in the sky on the day you were born.

There are twelve different signs, which are also part of four special groups.

Aries	Taurus	Gemini
March 21— April 19 (The Ram)	April 20— May 20 (The Bull)	May 21— June 21 (The Twins)
Libra	**Scorpio**	**Sagittarius**
 September 23— October 23 (The Scales)	October 24— November 21 (The Scorpion)	 November 22— December 21 (The Archer)

Air signs
Often curious, people born under air signs are good at making friends.

Water signs
These people are said to be sensitive and good at understanding people.

Fire signs
People born under fire signs are thought to be smart and strong.

Earth signs
Politeness and getting along with others are these signs' main qualities.

Cancer	Leo	Virgo
June 22— July 22 (The Crab)	July 23— August 22 (The Lion)	August 23— September 22 (The Maiden)
Capricorn	**Aquarius**	**Pisces**
December 22— January 19 (The Goat)	January 20— February 18 (The Water Bearer)	February 19— March 20 (The Fish)

Chinese horoscopes

Every New Year in China, one of **12 animals** is celebrated. It becomes that year's special animal and the **sign** of all the babies born that year.

Rat	Ox	Tiger
1984, 1996, 2008, 2020	**1985, 1997, 2009, 2021**	**1986, 1998, 2010, 2022**
Clever, funny, kind, and confident.	Hard-working, smart, and honest.	Brave, strong, and fiercely independent.

Horse	Goat	Monkey
1990, 2002, 2014, 2026	**1991, 2003, 2015, 2027**	**1992, 2004, 2016, 2028**
Full of energy, kind, and happy.	Creative, gentle, honest, and dreamy.	Playful, funny, and clever.

Animal personalities

Some people believe your animal sign influences your personality. Find the **year of your birth** on the chart to see if the animal sounds like you.

The Chinese New Year festival is in either January or February when the New Moon appears in the sky. The celebrations can last for days!

Rabbit	Dragon	Snake

1987, 1999, 2011, 2023 Gentle, kind, clever, and patient.	**1988, 2000, 2012, 2024** Powerful, confident, and very lucky.	**1989, 2001, 2013, 2025** Calm, chatty, wise, and thoughtful.

Rooster	Dog	Pig

1993, 2005, 2017, 2029 Honest, confident, and observant.	**1994, 2006, 2018, 2030** Friendly, happy, loyal, and brave.	**1995, 2007, 2019, 2031** Smart, generous, polite, and kind.

Precious gems

Beautiful and rare, gemstones come from rocks within the Earth, but it takes lots of time and effort to make them look pretty.

This is what some gems look like before being **CUT, CLEANED, and SHAPED.**

Cut gems sparkle because they have lots of facets (surfaces) that reflect light.

Rough ruby

Rough diamond

Rough emerald

Diamond

Citrine

Heliodor

Rose quartz

Topaz

Garnet

Fire opal

Ruby

Amethyst

Spinel

Sapphire

Apatite

Peridot

Tourmaline

Emerald

Jade

Cool clouds

Big and puffy or long and wispy, there are lots of different types of cloud drifting through the sky.

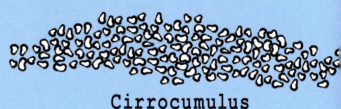

Cirrocumulus
(sir-oh-Kyoo-myuh-luhs)

Altocumulus
(al-toh-Kyoo-myuh-luhs)

Altostratus
(al-toh-strat-uhs)

All clouds are made of little drops of water or ice.

Stratocumulus
(strat-oh-Kyoo-myuh-luhs)

Stratus
(strat-uhs)

Stratocumulus   Cumulonimbus   Altocumulus

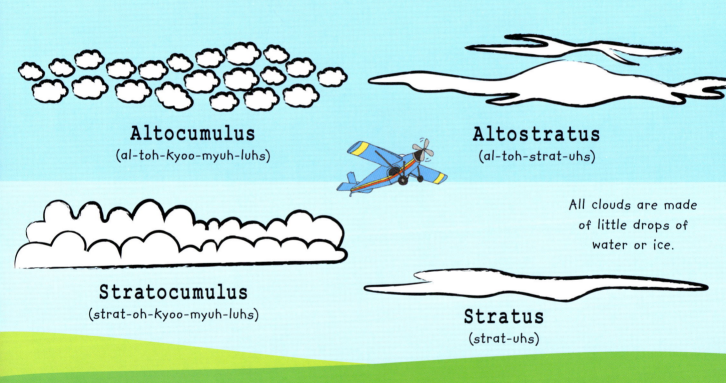

Cirrus
(sir-uhs)

Cumulonimbus
(Kyoo-myuh-loh-nim-buhs)

High
Above 20,000ft
(Above 6,000m)

Have you ever looked
up and seen **SHAPES**
in the clouds?

Cumulonimbus
clouds can
bring thunder
and lightning.

Medium
6,500ft—20,000ft
(2,000m—6,000m)

Cumulus
(Kyoo-myuh-luhs)

Low
Below 6,500ft
(Below 2,000m)

Altostratus

Cirrocumulus

Cirrus

Musical instruments

To make music you need an **instrument** (or your voice!). Instruments are sometimes put in groups based on how they make sound.

Bugle

Some instruments have strings.

Violin

Trumpet

Banjo

Ukulele

Tuba

String

Brass

Pan flute

You blow into brass and woodwind instruments to make sounds.

Drum

Electric keyboard

Recorder

Accordion

Cymbals

Saxophone

Tambourine

Piano

Working vehicles

Our roads, fields, and building sites are full of vehicles, but one of these might be needed if there's a special job to do.

Recycling
truck

Crane

Cranes are used
to build things.

ATV

Harvester

Ambulances take sick people to the hospital.

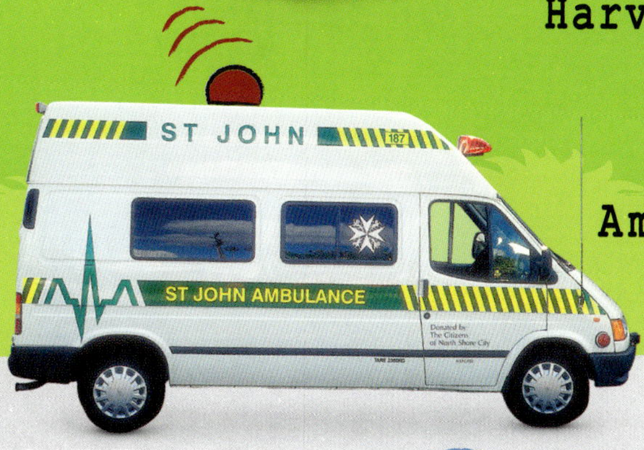

Ambulance

Police car

Fire engine

POLICE

Dump truck

Bulldozer

Beetle box

Found in a huge variety of colors, shapes, and sizes, beetles are some of the prettiest and most colorful creatures on Earth.

There are more than 350,000 different types of beetle.

Hercules beetle

Goliath beetle

Long feelers

Longhorn beetle

Stag beetle

Click beetle

Giraffe weevil

June bug

Scarab beetle

Did you know that most beetles have two pairs of wings?

Hairy jewel
beetle

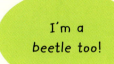

I'm a
beetle too!

Ladybug

Scarlet lily
beetle

Hard outer
wings protect
the pair they
fly with.

Gold beetle

Tortoise beetle

Jewel weevil

Violin beetle

Firefly

Namib desert
beetle

Discover **dinosaurs**

Here are some of the remarkable reptiles that walked the Earth millions of years ago.

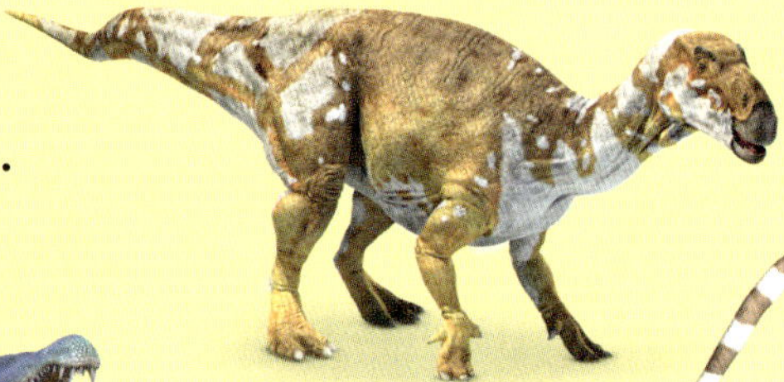

Iguanodon
(ig-GWAH-no-don)

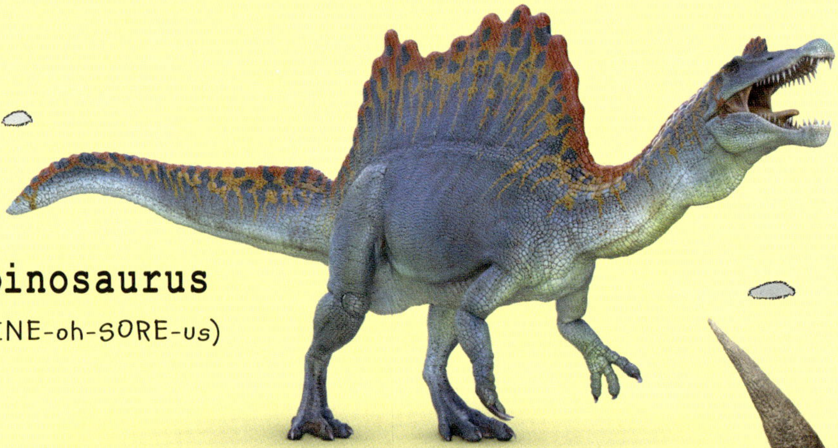

Spinosaurus
(SPINE-oh-SORE-us)

Big horns were probably used to attract a mate.

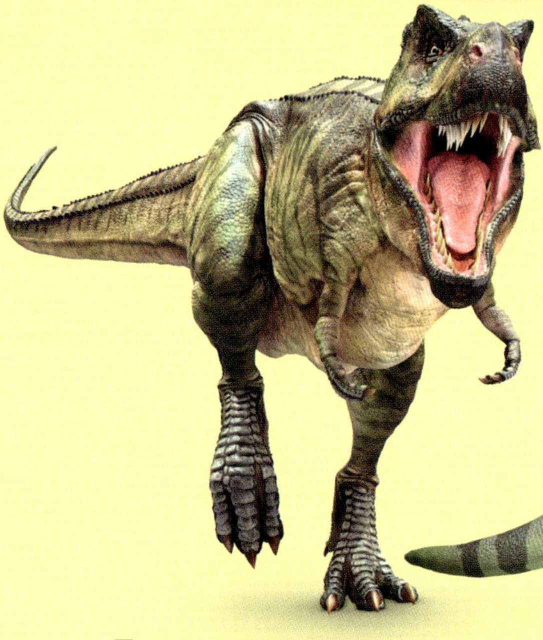

Tyrannosaurus
(TIE-ran-oh-SORE-us)

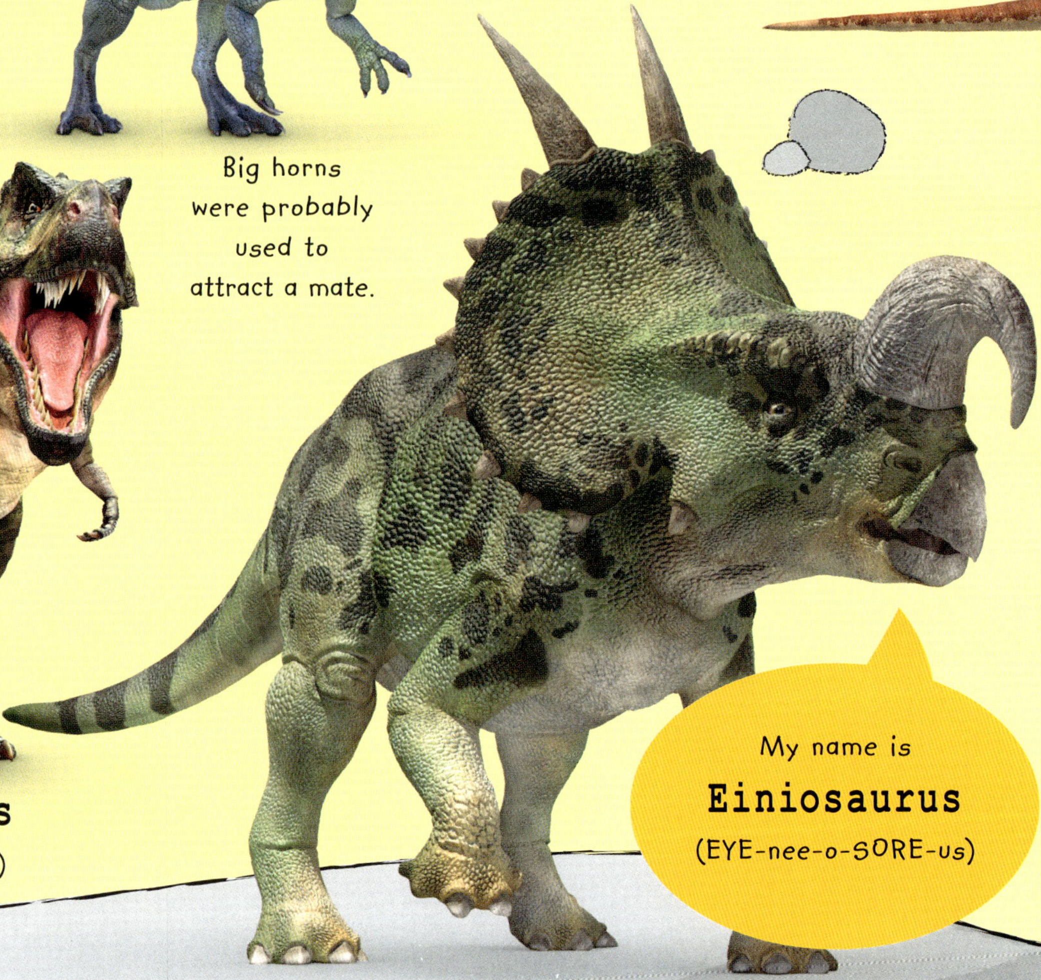

My name is
Einiosaurus
(EYE-nee-o-SORE-us)

Barosaurus
(BAH-roe-SORE-us)

Diplodocus
(dip-LOD-oh-kus)

Pachycephalosaurus
(PACK-ee-SEF-ah-low-SORE-us)

This giant was almost as long as three buses!

Dreadnoughtus
(dread-NOUGHT-iss)

Scientists think the Dreadnoughtus is one of the biggest land animals to have ever lived.

Stegosaurus
(STEG-oh-SORE-us)

Sauropelta
(SORE-oh-PELT-ah)

Extraordinary eggs

All **baby birds** hatch out of an egg. But bird eggs come in all different shapes, sizes, and colors.

Chicken

Song thrush

Cuckoo

Great auks are extinct. They died out nearly 200 years ago.

Great auk

Quail

Kiwi eggs are so big that they weigh a quarter of the mother's weight.

Kiwi

Golden eagle

King penguin

Peregrine falcon

Cormorant

Some eggs are pointy at one end so they don't roll off the sides of cliffs.

Tawny owl

Sparrowhawk

Dunnock

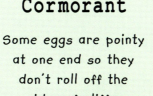

Hummingbird

Reptiles, fish, amphibians, and invertebrates also lay eggs!

I'm the BIGGEST bird in the world so I have the biggest eggs.

Emu

Ostrich

Animal babies

Baby animals and their parents don't always look the same. Some do, and many look quite similar, but some look nothing alike at all!

Butterfly

Ostrich

Tiger

Cub

Caterpillar

Owl

Owlet

Chick

Gorilla

Infant

Tapir

Calf

Fox

Tortoise

Penguin

Hatchling

Cub

Chick

Frog

Tadpole

Fantastic flags

Every country has a flag to use as a symbol of who they are. The design of most flags has a very special meaning.

Organizations, such as the Olympics and the United Nations can also have flags.

United Nations flag →

United Kingdom

Sweden

China

South Korea

Germany

Portugal

India

Malaysia

France

The Netherlands

Japan

Nepal

Spain

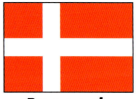
Denmark

Asia

Europe

212

United States of America

Brazil

Australia

South Africa

Canada

Ecuador

New Zealand

Egypt

Cuba

Chile

Samoa

Morocco

Mexico

Uruguay

Fiji

Algeria

Jamaica

Argentina

Tonga

Nigeria

North America

South America

Australia and the Pacific

Africa

Top 10: Countries

There are lots of countries in the world.
Some are **HUGE**, and others are small.

Saint Basil's Cathedral in Moscow, Russia

The top 10...
LARGEST countries

These countries are so big, you may have to take a plane to get from one side to the other!

1. Russia
2. Canada
3. China
4. United States of America
5. Brazil
6. Australia
7. India
8. Argentina
9. Kazakhstan
10. Algeria

American flag

Christ the Redeemer statue in Brazil

Australia

You could fit more than **38 MILLION** Vatican Cities into the space of Russia!

Saint Peter's Basilica in the Vatican City

The top 10...
SMALLEST countries

These countries don't have much space. You can walk through some of them in less than a day!

1. Vatican City
2. Monaco
3. Nauru
4. Tuvalu
5. San Marino
6. Liechtenstein
7. Marshall Islands
8. Saint Kitts and Nevis
9. Maldives
10. Malta

Tower in San Marino

Formula One car in Monaco

Vervet monkey on Saint Kitts

Beach in the Maldives

Top 10:World

Our world is full of amazing sights, from rivers that flow on and on, to huge deserts.

The top 10... LONGEST rivers

These huge rivers are SO long that some flow through lots of countries.

1. Nile, Africa
2. Amazon, South America
3. Yangzte, China
4. Mississippi, USA
5. Yenisei, Russia
6. Yellow River, China
7. Ob, Russia
8. Paraná, South America
9. Congo, Africa
10. Amur, Asia

Caiman

Piranha

The Amazon

A boat sailing along the Nile

It's hard to measure the size of deserts, as some are getting **BIGGER** and **BIGGER**.

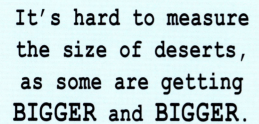
Penguin in Antarctica

The top 10...
LARGEST deserts

These dry places don't get much (or any) rain, and go on far further than the eye can see.

1. Antarctica
2. Arctic
3. Sahara, Africa
4. Arabian, Western Asia
5. Gobi, Asia
6. Patagonian, Argentina
7. Great Victoria, Australia
8. Kalahari, Africa
9. Great Basin, USA
10. Syrian, Syria

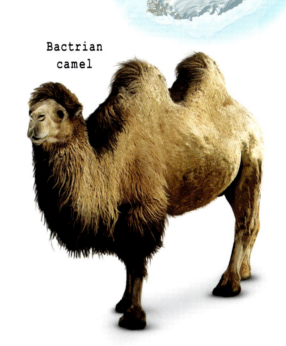
Bactrian camel

The Sahara

Top 10: Animals

Some animals may be dangerous to us, but protecting all animal species is very important.

Mosquitoes can carry deadly diseases.

Mosquito

Ten DEADLY animals

It's best to steer clear of these animals. They may have a fierce bite, deadly poison, or can spread disease.

Black mamba (snake)
Black widow (spider)
Blue-ringed octopus
Box jellyfish
Bullet ant
Great white shark
Hippopotamus
Mosquito
Poison dart frog
Tarantula hawk wasp

Great white shark

I'm very strong, fast, and aggressive.

Poison dart frog

Hippopotamus

Tarantula hawk wasp

Blue-ringed octopus

Giant panda

GOOD NEWS!
There weren't many pandas left a few years ago, but now their numbers are rising.

Black rhino

Ten ENDANGERED animals

Some animals are at risk of becoming extinct in the future. But luckily some people are trying to fix the problem.

I live in rain forests, but too many are being cut down.

Orangutan

Ring-tailed lemur

Black rhino

Hawaiian duck

Amur leopard

Siberian tiger

African penguin

Orangutan

Ring-tailed lemur

Golden poison frog

Malagasy giant rat

Radiated tortoise

Golden poison frog

Siberian tiger cub

Radiated tortoise

Index

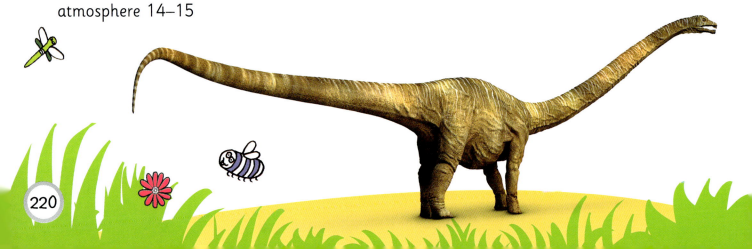

Acknowledgments

The publisher would like to thank the following for their kind permission to reproduce their photographs:

Key: a= above; b=below/bottom; c=center; f=far; l=left; r=right; t=top.
© Jerry Young: 56bl, 84c, 89bl, 100bl, 101c. 123RF.com: Liu Feng/long10000: 112bc; Eduardo Rivero / edurivero 179tc; sabphoto c; Erwin Wodicka / ginasanders 215tr. Alamy: NOAA 19tl; Gary Cook 123; Chad Ehlers 51tc; D. Hurst 151br; Martin Strmiska 67br; Sergey Uryadnikov 98–99c; domonabike 115cr; Lanmas 127clb; Dinodia Photos RM 130cl; Everett Collection Inc 130cra. Brand X Pictures / Alamy: Brian Hagiwara 174cra, 205tc. Corbis: 77tr, 127tl, crb; Don Hammond/ Design Pics 224r; Frank Krahmer/Radius Images 26–27; Micro Discover 148tr; Ocean 6bc; Viewstock 132–133t. © Philip Dowell: 127bl. Dorling Kindersley: Peter Anderson / Odds Farm Park, Buckinghamshire 83cr; Blackpool Zoo, Lancashire, UK 49br, 80br, 81cr, 81tl; British Wildlife Centre, Surrey, UK 211cr; Alan Burger 81tl; Claire Cordier 36bl; Bethany Dawn 34br; Greg and Yvonne Dean 100cl; Colin Keates / Natural History Museum, London 196bl, 205bl; Barnabas Kindersley 181br, 200c; Dave King / The Science Museum, London 109tr; Dave King / Booth Museum of Natural History, Brighton 65bl; Twan Leenders 73c, 73tl, 186bc, 186br, 219c; Liberty's Owl, Raptor and Reptile Centre, Hampshire, UK 80tc; James Mann / National Motor Museum Beaulieu 215c; Thomas Marent 216cr; NASA: 10cl, 16cr, 131cra, br, 143c, crb; Stephen Oliver 145tc, 160c, 160cr, 174tl, 201cl; Gary Ombler / The Real Aeroplane Company 136br; Gary Ombler / Nationaal Luchtvaart Themapark Aviodome 105tc, 136br; Gary Ombler / Vikings of Middle England 118br, 118bc, 119bl, 119br; Gary Ombler / Doubleday Swineshead Depot 203tc; Gary Ombler / Hastings Borough Council 123cr; Gary Ombler / University of Pennsylvania Museum of Archaeology and Anthropology 112cr, 121bc, 123cr; Gary Ombler / Zoe Doubleday-Collishaw, Swineshead Depot 132bc; Tim Parmenter / Natural History Museum, London 174c, 174tc, 197tl, 197tcl, 197br. Linda Pitkin 19tl; Wildlife Heritage Foundation, Kent, UK 99br; Jerry Young 8tl, 80c. James Stevenson / National Maritime Museum, London 119cr; Goddard Space Flight Center 129cr. Dreamstime.com: Carol Buchanan / Cbpix 66c; Jakub Cejpek / Jakupcejpek 85br; Torian Dixon / Mrincredible 130tr, 131tr, 131tc; Eric Isselee 101cl; Isselee 100cr, 186c, 186cr; Laumerle 46br; Mauhorng 152cr; Ollirg 62br; Pixworld 96br; Rosinka 12c; Wan Rosli Wan Othman / Rosliothman 116br, 117br; Darryn Schneider / Darryns 27br; Vladimir Seliverstov / Vladsilver 80tr; Staphy 57br; Jens Stolt / Jpsdk 77tl; Jan Martin Will / Freezingpictures 43bc, 81bl; Simone Winkler / Eyecatchlight 80tc; Yulia87 30–31 (background); Thomas Lenne 130bl; Vjanez 130bc; Photka 130br; Isselee 219cb. FLPA: Frans Lanting 69tl; Harri Taavetti 84–85cra. Fotolia: Andreas Altenburger / arrxxx 89cr; Kitch Bain 181tc; Beboy 22c; HD Connelly 104cra; DM7 62bl; dundanim 8bc, 10bc, 171bc; Eric Isselee 65bc, 218br, 219tl, 219cr, 219br; Pekka Jaakkola / Luminis 137tr; Valeriy Kalyuzhnyy / StarJumper 155br; Dariusz Kopestynski 113bl; Yahia Loukkal 203bl; Steve Lovegrove 87bl, 217bc; Kevin Moore 98c; Olena Pantiukh 69bl; Strezhnev Pavel 79tc; rolffimages 36bc, 92cr; Dario Sabljak 144tc, 164br; Silver 57tr; uwimages

67bc; Alex Vasilev 83bc. Getty: Tom Brakefield / Photodisc 80bc; Don Farrall / Digital Vision 67tl; Frank Krahmer / Photographer's Choice 85tl; MIXA 53tc; Photographer's Choice RF / Jon Boyes 170br; Rolling Earth 78; David Tipling / Digital Vision 81tc. Getty Images: Steve Bronstein 141bl; Don Farrall / Photodisc 59br, 89cl; Hulton Archive 127cra; Javier Fernández Sánchez 97tr; Michael & Patricia Fogden 96tl; Dave and Les Jacobs 138cl; Ingo Jezierski / Photodisc 112cl; Ralph Martin / BIA 97ca; Tse Hon Ning 155bc; Alastair Pollock Photography 97cb; Anup Shah 97c; Universal Images Group 126cb; Vladimir Zakharov 139cr; Peter Zelei Images 138cl/shard; zhuyongming 139c. Shutterstock.com: Dayat Banggai 127fclb; Yeti Crab 128cr; Route66 128br. Philippe Giraud © Dorling Kindersley: 4bc. Ellen Howdon © Dorling Kindersley, Courtesy of Glasgow Museum: 128bc. iStockphoto.com: id-work (194–195all); pop_jop 175 cla, 212–213 (UK, Sweden, Spain, USA, South Africa, Samoa, Uruguay, Tonga, China, Brazil, Australia, Canada, Cuba, Chile, Algeria, Argentina, Portugal, Malaysia, Netherlands, New Zeland, Morocco, Mexico, Nigeria Germany, South Korea, India, France, Japan, Denmark, Ecuador, Egypt, Fiji). Kohn Pedersen Fox: 139cl/Lotte. Richard Leeney © Dorling Kindersley, Courtesy of Search and Rescue Hovercraft, Richmond, British Columbia: 16c. NASA: 14crb, 42bl, 141br, 141rl, 142bl, 195tr. Gary Ombler © Dorling Kindsersley, Courtesy of Cotswold Wildlife Park: 211tc. Gary Ombler © Dorling Kindersley, Courtesy of the Board of Trustees of the Royal Armouries: 93bc. Photolibrary: Corbis 73cr, 105tr, 137tr; Photodisc / Photolink 141tl. PunchStock: Photodisc / Paul Souders 27br; Stockbyte 201cr. James Stevenson © Dorling Kindersley, Courtesy of the National Maritime Museum, London: 126cl.

Jacket images: Front: Dorling Kindersley: Jerry Young bcr.

DK would like to thank:
Carrie Love for editorial assistance and proofreading. Elinor Greenwood, Carrie Lewis, Andrea Mills, Syed Tuba Javed, and Robin Moul for additional editorial work. Anita Ganeri for fact checking. Martin Copeland, Laura Evans, Rob Nunn, Nishwan Rasool and Lee Thompson for picture library assistance.